SHARING THE
JOURNEY

*The Passover seder is a
shared Jewish experience
that has historical and
contemporary significance
to persons of all faiths.*

SHARING THE JOURNEY

The Haggadah for
the Contemporary Family

Written by Alan S. Yoffie   Illustrated by Mark Podwal

Rabbi Mary L. Zamore, Consulting Editor

CENTRAL CONFERENCE OF AMERICAN RABBIS

Library of Congress Cataloging-in-Publication Data

Haggadah (Reform, Yoffie). English & Hebrew.

Sharing the journey : the Haggadah for the contemporary family / written by Alan S. Yoffie ; illustrated by Mark Podwal ; Mary L. Zamore, consulting editor.

    p. cm.

  English and Hebrew.

  Includes bibliographical references.

  ISBN 978-0-88123-183-0 (pbk. : alk. paper) — ISBN 978-0-88123-185-4 (deluxe hardcover : alk. paper)

  1. Haggadot—Texts. 2. Seder—Liturgy—Texts. 3. Reform Judaism—Liturgy—Texts. I. Yoffie, Alan S., 1945– II. Podwal, Mark H., 1945– III. Zamore, Mary L., 1969– IV. Title.
BM674.74.Y74 2012
296.4'5—dc23

2011046376

Every effort has been made to ascertain the owners of copyrights for the selections used in this volume and to obtain permission to reprint copyrighted material. The CCAR will be pleased, in subsequent editions, to correct any inadvertent errors or omissions. The Central Conference of American Rabbis expresses its gratitude for the permissions received, as follows:

Jewish Publication Society: Psalms reprinted from *Tanakh: The New JPS Translation to the Traditional Hebrew Text* © 1985 by the Jewish Publication Society. Used with the permission of the publisher.

Susan Horowitz: Hineih Mah Tov © Sue Horowitz, 2006. Used by permission of the artist.

10 9 8 7 6 5 4 3

CCAR Press
New York, New York
ccarpress.org

Book design by Rebecca S. Neimark, Twenty-Six Letters
www.twentysixletters.com

Rabbi Barton and Jane Shallat
are honored to dedicate this Haggadah
to our grandchildren,
Zachary, Sean, and Jordan Shallat.
May they always be wise.

CONTENTS

The Meal Is Served

Concluding the Seder

FOREWORD

It has been my privilege to encourage Alan Yoffie's vision for this Haggadah and to foster his desire to create a truly welcoming seder experience. As he reminds us, "The story of the Exodus is not just a Jewish story. It is a story that embodies humanity's passion for justice and freedom."

Indeed, each individual present at the seder, whether raised in Judaism or in another faith tradition, brings valuable wisdom, insights, and questions to the exploration of the true meaning of Passover. "In every generation each individual is bound to regard himself or herself as if he or she had personally gone forth from Egypt." In Yoffie's words, it is not "each Jew" but "each individual" who must reflect upon leaving Egypt.

Sharing the Journey encourages us to be sensitive to the unique personal and religious background each individual brings to the retelling of the Exodus story. This inclusive Haggadah enables everyone around the table to feel involved in the universal theme of the struggle for freedom, especially important for those having a first experience of attending or hosting a Passover seder.

"Because we were slaves in Egypt,"Judaism teaches we should "know the heart of the stranger" (Exodus 23:9). We must remember the experience of the outsider, those who are unfamiliar with particular customs and traditions. This Haggadah encourages all seder participants to "learn more about ourselves and each other and make the story of Passover our own."

Sharing the Journey acknowledges that Hebrew prayers may not be known by all and models inclusivity through its gender-sensitive language. It is also sensitive to the role women have played in redemption of all peoples. Yoheved, Moses's mother, Miriam, his sister, the Egyptian midwives Shiphrah and Puah, and even Pharoah's daughter are all credited with their rightful role as redeemers. Similarly, Zipporah, Moses's wife from a Midianite background, is cited for her insight and the part she played in saving the lives of Moses and their two sons (Exodus 4:24–26).

Alan Yoffie has emphasized the obligation for all of us "to strive to enhance our vigilance against injustice" and to do our part in freeing ourselves and others from oppression of any kind. Only when we recognize that which may shackle our own hearts and minds can we truly leave Egypt (*Mitzrayim* in Hebrew, literally: narrow places) and escape the "narrow places" that constrain our own humanity.

DR. PAULA J. BRODY
Outreach Training Institute, Director
Union for Reform Judaism/Reform Jewish Outreach Boston

PREFACE

Sharing the Journey: The Haggadah for the Contemporary Family is written to address the needs of every member of the contemporary Reform Jewish community, wherever you may be in your religious commitment or observances. The contemporary Jewish family may include those who are born Jewish, those who have chosen to be Jewish, and family members of other faiths. For those across the spectrum of knowledge, religious practice, and faith—from observant Reform Jews to those for whom Judaism and Jewish Festivals and traditions are new—this Haggadah provides a text for a joyful and inspirational family seder.

Sharing the Journey accomplishes its objectives by embracing traditions and clarifying the meaning of the symbols and rituals of Passover in language that is clear and approachable. For guests who are attending their first seder or who do not know what questions to ask about the observance of Passover, *Sharing the Journey* provides clarity to the seder ceremony and an opportunity for a meaningful seder experience. For those whose participation in a seder is an important religious occasion, *Sharing the Journey* provides an opportunity to gain a deeper understanding of God's teachings through the story of the Exodus. For everyone, *Sharing the Journey* provides an opportunity to learn more about the Jewish people's struggle for freedom.

The Passover seder has traditionally comprised fourteen sections. *Sharing the Journey* uses the traditional order of the seder as a template. Blessings, prayers, and stories historically read or recited at the seder are contained in this Haggadah. So that all family members and guests feel welcome to the joyous celebration of freedom, new inclusive language has also been added. In order to encourage participation in the whole seder, some sections and material from traditional Haggadah texts have been shortened or omitted. Some of these passages are found in the appendix, however, and may be inserted into the service at the discretion of the seder leader. To capture the full meaning of the text, some

Hebrew passages have been translated creatively in the Haggadah rather than literally.

Seders, as well as the Haggadot read at seders, have evolved over the centuries in response to changed realities. The welcoming of family and friends, the lighting and blessing of Festival candles, a prayer to give thanks, and the blessing of children have been included at the beginning of the seder. More contemporary additions to the modern seder include a remembrance of the Holocaust and recognition of the role played by Miriam, the sister of Moses, in the story of the Exodus. These innovations to the seder service are included in *Sharing the Journey*.

"A Passover Checklist" reviews the Passover symbols needed to conduct the seder and provides a few notes for the seder leader, helpful hints for preparation of the seder table, and other information regarding the holiday.

Passover is the Jewish holiday that typically generates many wonderful family memories and experiences. *Sharing the Journey* is written to help all members of the contemporary Jewish family create a joyous and inspirational Passover experience.

ACKNOWLEDGMENTS

Sharing the Journey: The Haggadah for the Contemporary Family would not have been possible without the support and encouragement of many persons.

Special thanks go to Dr. Paula Brody, Director of the Outreach Training Institute, URJ Reform Jewish Outreach, Boston, MA and Rabbi Matthew Berger of Temple Emanuel in Worcester, MA. Wonderful programs at the Outreach Training Institute supplied inspiration for *Sharing the Journey*. Dr. Brody provided many insightful comments on the early drafts and graciously suggested other "Readers" who provided valuable feedback. Rabbi Berger met with me on many occasions to discuss the manuscript and responded to many emails in the midst of a very busy rabbinic schedule. I am grateful for the wealth of knowledge that he shared.

Special thanks also go to Rabbi Hara Person, Publisher and Director of the CCAR Press, and Mark Podwal. Rabbi Person directed an inclusive process that brought the Haggadah from raw manuscript to finished product. She did so with great professionalism, patience, and, always, an upbeat nature which was much appreciated. Mark Podwal's illustrations add great beauty and visual commentary to *Sharing the Journey*. Mark listened to ideas and graciously shared his creative thinking as he executed his magnificent illustrations.

I was privileged to have the support of a very special group of Readers:

VICKY FARHI, Outreach Specialist in the Congregational Consulting Group of the Union for Reform Judaism;

JIM KEEN, author of *Inside Intermarriage, A Christian Partner's Perspective on Raising a Jewish Family* (URJ Press);

MARTIN SLEEPER, PHD, Associate Executive Director, Facing History and Ourselves, Brookline, MA;

JOYCE SCHWARTZ, Director of Outreach & Ambassador Programs, URJ Reform Jewish Outreach, Boston, MA; and

MICHAEL D. SLEEPER and CARLTON WATSON, former Presidents of Temple Emanuel, Worcester, MA, friends and laymen dedicated to Judaism and the Jewish community.

I am thankful to each of my Readers for providing me with the benefit of their knowledge and experiences.

By celebrating Passover we keep alive Jewish traditions and pass on the lessons of the story of the Exodus to our children, our families, and our guests. My parents, William A. Yoffie and Judith S. Yoffie, and the parents of Jody (my wife), Rabbi Herbert E. Drooz and Florence Z. Drooz, understood the special significance of the celebration of Passover and passed that knowledge on to their children and to their grandchildren. We shall always remember them for their wisdom and their love and shall be forever grateful. Jody and I are also especially proud of our children, Alexandra Yoffie Sleeper, Nathan Sleeper and their family, Victoria S. Yoffie, Abraham S. Yoffie, and Isadora S. Yoffie. Each year they re-experience our Exodus from Egypt at our family seders and continue to bring us joy.

For Passover 2010, my family's seders were conducted using an early draft of *Sharing the Journey*. The comments about the new Haggadah on the first night of Passover and the more vigorous questions and commentary at the second seder the following evening provided valuable perspective on what was required to complete the manuscript. Special thanks go to Michael and Carol Sleeper and their children, and to David and Marlene Persky, Lillian Cohen Eisenberg and Lawrence Cohen, all family members who shared their insight and with whom we have enjoyed so many Passover celebrations. Thanks also to David Greenberg, an active participant in our seders at 100 years old whose comments and complements will always be cherished, and to the many others, both Jewish and those of other faiths, who have participated in our yearly seders and added to our joy and learning.

I am also grateful to:

NANETTE STAHL, Curator of the Judaica Collection at the Yale University Library, who created a connection for me with Mark Podwal, graciously shared her knowledge and provided access to many of the beautiful Haggadot, in the Yale University collection;

HENRY A. HEIMAN, ESQUIRE of Wilmington, DE and Geoffrey Dellenbaugh, Esquire, Professor of intellectual property law at the University of Connecticut School of Law, who provided me advice regarding legal issues and who were so helpful; and

PETER and ELLEN ALLARD, wonderful performers and composers, who provided me with suggestions about music for the Haggadah when it was still in its formative stages.

Others who made contributions for which I am thankful include: Rabbi Steven A. Fox, Chief Executive, CCAR; Rabbi Elaine S. Zecher, Chair of the CCAR Worship and Practice Committee, Rabbi Joel L. Sisenwine, CCAR Chair of Joint Commission on Worship and Music, Consulting Editor, Rabbi Mary Zamore, and Rabbi Richard S. Sarason, Professor of Rabbinic Literature and Thought at the HUC-JIR, Cincinnati, OH, who reviewed the manuscript and made thoughtful recommendations; CCAR Rabbinic Intern and Music Editor Josh Beraha; Cantor Joshua Breitzer and Rabbi Sarah Reines who recorded the music for *Sharing the Journey,* their engaging voices encouraging everyone to participate in song, contributing to the inclusive experience of the seder; Cantor Lanie Katzew; Victor Ney; Michael Goldberg; Mike Boxer; Steve Brodsky; CCAR staff members Debbie Smilow and Ortal Bensky; designer Rebecca Neimark; copy editor Debra Hirsch Corman, and proofreaders Leslie Rubin and Michelle Kwitkin-Close.

Finally, I dedicate *Sharing the Journey* to my wife, Johanna D. Drooz Yoffie. The writing of the Haggadah would not have been possible without Jody's support and encouragement. Jody fills my life with joy and hope for the future. Her love and her commitment to family and to Judaism continue to inspire all who know her "all the days of our lives." I am a lucky man!

ALAN S. YOFFIE
Worcester, MA
January 2012

A PASSOVER CHECKLIST

Preparation for the Seder

The Seder Plate

The seder plate displays the central symbols of Passover. Specially designed plates may be purchased online, at stores selling Judaica, and frequently at congregational gift shops. They may also be made at home. The seder plate is traditionally placed in front of the seder leader and contains the following items:

A Green Vegetable (page 24)

In Hebrew, *karpas* (כַּרְפַּס). Often parsley. Cilantro, celery, or other green vegetables may also be used. During the seder, we say a blessing and eat the *karpas*, which represents the "fruit of the earth." In some cold-weather countries, like those in Eastern Europe, a potato was substituted when a green vegetable was not available at Passover. A potato is still used to represent the fruit of the earth at some seders today.

Bitter Herbs (page 57)

In Hebrew, *maror* (מָרוֹר). Generally horseradish root and/or grated horseradish. We say a blessing and eat the *maror* so that we never forget the bitterness and oppression of slavery.

Some seder plates have a spot for a second bitter herb. When two herbs are present on the plate, we say a blessing and "dip" one herb—romaine lettuce, endive, or other bitter vegetable (see page 57)—and we mix horseradish with *charoset* for making the Hillel sandwich (see page 58).

Charoset (page 57)

In Hebrew, *charoset* (חֲרֹסֶת). *Charoset* is a sweet condiment that reminds us of the mortar used by slaves in Egypt to build monuments.

Charoset is usually made in the home. Historically, the specific ingredients depended on what was available locally. Ashkenazi recipes (recipes

of families from Central and Eastern Europe) typically blend diced apples and nuts with sweet red wine. Many Sephardi recipes (recipes of families descended from the Spanish Jewish community) use a variety of mashed dried fruits. Persian Jews, from what is now Iran, make *charoset* with pistachios, dates, bananas, pomegranate, and cardamon. Venetian *charoset* is made with chestnut paste, figs, poppy seeds, dried apricots, almonds, and brandy.

ROASTED EGG (PAGE 25)

In Hebrew, *beitzah* (בֵּיצָה). On the seder plate, the roasted egg symbolizes the promise of new life and the ongoing cycle of life and renewal. The egg is also a reminder of the days of the ancient Temple in Jerusalem, when Festival offerings were brought to the Temple during Passover.

ROASTED SHANK BONE (PAGE 48)

In Hebrew, *z'roa* (זְרוֹעַ). On the seder plate, the roasted shank bone, usually of a lamb, serves as a reminder that God passed over our houses (marked with lamb's blood) when God afflicted Egypt with the tenth plague, the slaying of the firstborn. A shank bone can generally be obtained from a local butcher.

Historically, the shank bone represents the *pesach* (paschal lamb) and *chagigah* (festival offering) sacrifices performed in the ancient Temple in Jerusalem. Since the destruction of the Temple in 70 CE by the Romans, Jews have been forbidden to eat these sacrifices on Passover. (Lamb, therefore, is not served at the seder.)

OTHER SYMBOLS THAT MAY BE FOUND ON A CONTEMPORARY SEDER PLATE

A RED BEET

The Rabbis of the Talmud (*P'sachim* 114b) suggest the use of a beet as a substitute for a shank bone. Though their reasoning has nothing to do with vegetarianism, today a beet is often used as a vegetarian substitute. When the symbol of the shank bone is discussed during the seder, the seder leader instead raises the beet from the seder plate.

AN ORANGE

Sometimes an orange is added to the seder plate. The use of this symbol was originated by Dr. Susannah Heschel, a feminist scholar, to show solidarity with gays and lesbians. The orange was selected to represent the additional fruitfulness of a society that welcomes and includes members with diverse sexual orientations.

ADDITIONAL SEDER SYMBOLS

WINE
During the seder, we say a blessing over and drink four cups of kosher wine, representing the fruit of the vine. For children and those who do not drink wine, grape juice is an acceptable substitute.

MATZAH
Matzah, unleavened bread, is eaten in place of bread during Passover. During our seder, we say a blessing over and then eat matzah, which symbolizes our "bread of affliction."

HARD-BOILED EGGS
A Roman symbol of the cycle of life, hard-boiled eggs are frequently served at the beginning of the seder meal. Salt water is sometimes poured over the egg before eating. The egg and the salt water combine the symbol for the renewal of life with the tears of slavery.

PILLOW
For the chair of the seder leader or anyone else who wants one. The pillow is a symbol for freedom. Historically, slaves sat on hard benches or on the floor when they ate. For the early Greeks, reclining on low couches while eating from trays was a sign of a free person. Once tables and chairs were the more common way to eat, the custom became to use pillows instead of couches. The Rabbis adapted this custom for the seder.

SETTING THE PASSOVER TABLE

TWO CANDLESTICKS, TWO CANDLES, AND MATCHES (PAGE 17)
For lighting of the Festival candles. Historically, candle lighting (lighting the candles and reciting the blessing) was a woman's responsibility. Today, men and women, as well as children, may participate equally in this ritual.

A WINE GLASS FOR EACH PERSON AND DECANTERS/BOTTLES OF WINE AT EACH TABLE (PAGE 21)
For *Kiddush*—the blessing of the "fruit of the vine." We drink the wine and say a blessing four times during the seder.

A PITCHER OF WATER, A SMALL BOWL, AND A TOWEL (PAGE 23)
For the washing of hands by the seder leader. Those at the seder table may also wash their hands or symbolically join with the leader/reader.

BOWL(S) FOR *KARPAS*/A GREEN VEGETABLE AND BOWL(S) OF SALT WATER (PAGE 24)
For blessing of the fruit of the earth. Before the blessing of the *karpas*/ fruit of the earth, each person takes a piece of parsley/greens and dips it

in salt water. If there is a large group at the seder table, it is helpful (and facilitates the progress of the seder) to have several small bowls with parsley and several small bowls of salt water to pass around the table.

A Plate with Three Pieces of Matzah: The Upper Matzah, Middle Matzah, and Bottom Matzah (page 25)

For the breaking of the middle matzah. Three pieces of matzah are on the table in front of the seder leader. The three matzahs are separately covered or may be placed in a special "matzah cover" that is divided into three parts. Matzah covers are sold online, at stores selling Judaica, and frequently at congregational gift shops. Making a matzah cover at home can be a good way to involve children in preparations for the seder.

Napkin for Wrapping and Hiding the Afikoman (page 25)

The *afikoman* is a piece of the middle matzah. During the seder, the middle matzah is broken, and the largest piece (the *afikoman*) is wrapped and hidden.

Plate(s) of Matzah (page 25)

For the blessing of matzah and for Hillel's sandwich. When discussing the "bread of affliction," each person takes a small piece of matzah and raises it when we read in unison. The matzah is then returned to the table and is eaten later in the seder after a blessing is recited.

Small Bowl(s) of Charoset (page 57)

For Hillel's sandwich. *Charoset* is mixed with *maror* (bitter herbs/horseradish) and placed on matzah to make Hillel's sandwich.

Miriam's Cup and Water Glasses (page 45)

For the ritual honoring Miriam. One cup filled with water is raised by the seder leader during the ritual of Miriam's cup. This cup may be specially designated or designed for this purpose, but any festive glass or goblet from the home may be used. As part of the ritual, each person drinks from Miriam's Cup or from their own water glasses.

Elijah's Cup (page 63)

For when we open the door for Elijah. A *Kiddush* (wine) cup, generally specially designated, but any attractive glass or goblet from the home may be used.

Pitcher(s) of Salt Water

If hard-boiled eggs are served to begin the meal, participants may wish to pour salt water over the egg before eating it. See above, "Hard-Boiled Eggs."

An Alternative Table Setting

In some communities, a common tradition is to provide everyone with a small plate setting containing a sprig of parsley, a hard-boiled egg, a spoonful of horseradish, and a spoonful of *charoset*.

The Search for Leaven *(Chameitz)*: A Family Activity Before the Seder

During Passover we eat matzah, unleavened bread. Grain products such as bread baked with yeast (foods that are already fermented) and ingredients that cause fermentation are not eaten during Passover. Foods that "have risen" are called *chameitz*, and ingredients, like yeast, that cause food to rise are called "leaven," or *s'or.*

In preparation for Passover, families search for and remove leaven and leavened products from their homes so that it will not be eaten accidentally during Passover. A ritual search for leaven representing the entire cleaning process takes place the night before the seder. Bread crumbs or wrapped pieces of bread are placed (or hidden for children to find) in crevices and other places in the home. Lights are turned off, and a candle (or flashlight) is used for the search. When the crumbs are found, they are swept up with a feather (the traditional method) or brush and dustpan (a modern substitute). After they are collected, the crumbs are kept in one place and burned the following morning in a safe place, such as a kitchen sink or outside on a grill.

Conducting the search and removing the leaven is a family activity that heightens anticipation for a joyous seder celebration. Young children especially enjoy this activity.

The following blessings and readings may be recited in unison by families when conducting the search and burning the leaven:

BLESSING BEFORE THE SEARCH BEGINS THE NIGHT BEFORE THE PASSOVER SEDER

בָּרוּךְ אַתָּה, יְיָ אֱלֹהֵינוּ, מֶלֶךְ הָעוֹלָם,
אֲשֶׁר קִדְּשָׁנוּ בְּמִצְוֹתָיו, וְצִוָּנוּ עַל בִּעוּר חָמֵץ.

*Baruch atah, Adonai Eloheinu, Melech haolam,
asher kid'shanu b'mitzvotav, v'tzivanu al biur chameitz.*

Blessed are You, Eternal our God, Sovereign of the universe,
who sanctifies us with Your commandments
and calls upon us to remove leaven.

AFTER THE SEARCH IS CONCLUDED

כָּל־חֲמִירָא וַחֲמִיעָא דְּאִכָּא בִרְשׁוּתִי דְּלָא חֲמִתֵּהּ וּדְלָא
בַעֲרִתֵּהּ לִבְטִיל וְלֶהֱוֵי כְּעַפְרָא דְאַרְעָא.

*Kol chamira vachamia d'ika virshuti d'la chamiteih ud'la
vaariteih livtil v'lehevei k'afra d'ara.*

Any leaven that is in my possession,
that I have not seen or not removed,
shall be unclaimed and considered as the dust of the earth.

BEFORE BURNING THE LEAVEN THE NEXT MORNING

כָּל־חֲמִירָא וַחֲמִיעָא דְּאִכָּא בִרְשׁוּתִי,
דַּחֲמִתֵּהּ וּדְלָא חֲמִתֵּהּ, דְּבַעֲרִתֵּהּ וּדְלָא בַעֲרִתֵּהּ,
לִבְטִיל וְלֶהֱוֵי כְּעַפְרָא דְאַרְעָא.

*Kol chamira vachamia d'ika virshuti,
dachamiteih ud'la chamiteih, d'vaariteih ud'la baariteih,
livtil v'lehevei k'afra d'ara.*

Any leaven that is in my possession, whether I have
seen it or not, whether I have removed it or not,
shall be unclaimed and considered as the dust of the earth.

A MOMENT FOR ADDITIONAL LEARNING

The commandment to eat only unleavened food on Passover comes from
the Torah (Exodus 12:15; Leviticus 23:6). In Jewish tradition, the differ-
ence between what is leavened and what is not extends beyond simply a
concern with food. The Rabbis of the Talmud use leaven as a metaphor
for the evil or unruly impulses in our hearts (BT *B'rachot* 17a), that which
we need to guard against. Historically, the specifics of what food may be
eaten and what is prohibited on Passover have been the subject of much
debate. Eating only matzah during Passover demonstrates our readiness
to serve God in joyous freedom from inner as well as outer bondage.

After the Passover Seder

PASSOVER IS CELEBRATED FOR SEVEN DAYS

Seven days is the period of time that the Torah instructs us to refrain
from eating leavened bread (Exodus 12:15; Leviticus 23:6). From as early
as the days of the ancient Temple in Jerusalem, however, Passover was

celebrated for eight days outside of Israel. In times when communication between areas was more difficult, determining the proper dates for the start of Jewish holidays using the lunar calendar was not always clear. As a result, for holiday observances outside of the Land of Israel, an extra day was added and a second seder conducted. In the nineteenth century, Reform Jews eliminated the extra day of observance, as its original rationale was no longer seen as valid. Today, the Reform Movement adheres to the same biblical time frame that is followed in the modern State of Israel. *Many Reform Jews, however, continue to observe the practice of participating in two seders.*

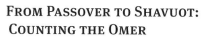

FROM PASSOVER TO SHAVUOT: COUNTING THE OMER

Passover celebrates the liberation from slavery in Egypt and our redemption by God more than three thousand years ago. The Passover seder, however, is just the beginning of our celebrations. The holiday of Shavuot celebrates God's giving the Torah to the Jewish people at Mount Sinai. It commemorates the day on which the Jewish people became a nation united in service to God. Shavuot comes exactly fifty days after our celebration of freedom from slavery. The counting of the days from the second night of Passover to sunset on Shavuot is called the period of the counting of the Omer. Passover comes at the time of the barley harvest in ancient Israel. Shavuot comes at the time of the ancient wheat harvest, and "omer" refers to a sheaf of barley. The counting of the Omer is a nightly reminder of the approach of the coming celebration. Traditionally, the celebration of Shavuot includes a public reading of the Ten Commandments, as well as the Book of Ruth. (Counting the Omer may be found in *Mishkan T'filah: A Reform Siddur,* page 570.)

A Few Notes for the Seder Leader

A SEDER IS a participatory ritual. Active participation by all family members and guests is encouraged.

WELCOME EVERYONE TO the seder table. Today, when family may be scattered across the country or the globe, a welcome is as appropriate for family members as for strangers. If some family members are not able to attend the seder in person, it may be possible for them to connect via the Internet for at least a portion of the seder.

IT IS HELPFUL to inform those attending their first seder that the service is conveniently divided into three parts—the service before the meal, the Passover meal, and the conclusion of the seder after the meal.

THE SEDER LEADER may read any section of the Haggadah himself/herself or delegate the reading to another person.

SOME FAMILY MEMBERS and guests may not be able to read (or prefer not to read) from the Haggadah. Inform everyone that they may "pass" when called upon to read or when it is their turn to be the "Reader."

BLESSINGS AND OTHER passages may be recited in either Hebrew or English or in both languages.

SOME KNOWLEDGE OF Hebrew is helpful but is not required for leading the service. English transliterations of Hebrew are provided for all the blessings, prayers, and songs. Transliterations, however, can be a challenge to read, especially at a first reading. A review of the transliterations prior to the seder will be helpful.

TRADITIONALLY, THE SEDER leader conducts the seder while "reclining" on a pillow on his/her chair. A pillow may also be used by anyone else who wants one (see page 3).

THE RICHNESS AND beauty of the illustrations in *Sharing the Journey* add visual commentary to the Passover story. Directing attention to illustrations throughout the seder may create opportunities for discussion and increased participation.

MUSIC FOR THE Passover blessings and songs in this Haggadah can be found on *Sharing the Journey: A Musical Seder Companion* and may be downloaded from various music download sites. The seder leader may choose to have family and guests sing along with the cantorial vocalists or with an instrumental version or simply chant the melody that is most familiar to their family. Both the cantorial and instrumental versions are available to download. The music selected is mostly traditional Jewish melodies. "Piggyback" songs (Passover lyrics applied to familiar secular melodies) and an African-American spiritual ("Go Down Moses")

are also included. Songs that can be found in the *Sharing the Journey: A Musical Seder Companion* are indicated by this icon: ♫.

What Matters on Passover Is That Questions Are Asked

During the Passover seder we are encouraged to ask questions and to discuss the contemporary significance of the story of the Exodus. *Sharing the Journey* provides an opportunity for asking questions during the seder. Opportunities are also provided to discuss the questions raised by the story of the Exodus. One or more of these questions may be selected for discussion each year. Families are also encouraged to compose their own questions for discussion.

QUESTIONS FOR DISCUSSION

MATZAH: A SYMBOL OF HOPE AND THE RESPONSIBILITIES OF FREEDOM (P. 27)
After reading about the symbolism of the second half of the middle matzah, the following questions may be asked: Who are those struggling for freedom today? What are the responsibilities of free persons?

LET US REMEMBER: THE HOLOCAUST (PAGE 28)
Elie Wiesel's comments when visiting Buchenwald in 2009 create an opportunity for a short discussion on the Holocaust and the reasons we have for being hopeful about the future:

> Memory has become a sacred duty of all people of good will. . . . When I was liberated (from Buchenwald) in 1945 . . . paradoxically, I was so hopeful then. Many of us were, although we had the right to give up on humanity, to give up on culture, to give up on education, to give up on the possibility of living one's life with dignity in a world that has no place for dignity. We rejected that possibility and we said, no, we must continue believing in the future.

REPLY TO THE FOUR QUESTIONS (PAGE 32)
After responding to why we use a pillow and recline when we eat during the Seder, the following question may be asked: What are other historical or current symbols of freedom?

THE TEN PLAGUES (PAGES 40–42)
After the recitation of the ten plagues, the following question may be asked: What are plagues we live with in our world today?

THE WATCH-NIGHT OF THE ETERNAL (PAGE 51)
After acknowledging that we are bound to live our lives "as if" God redeemed each of us from slavery, the following question may be asked: How does the idea of living our lives "as if" God brought us out of Egypt impact the decisions we make about what we do for others?

The Traditional Order of the Passover Seder

Sharing the Journey: The Haggadah for the Contemporary Family uses the traditional order of the seder as a template while also including new rituals and readings for the contemporary Jewish family.

קַדֵּשׁ

KADEISH

KIDDUSH: BLESSING OVER THE
FIRST CUP OF WINE

וּרְחַץ

URCHATZ

WASHING THE HANDS

כַּרְפַּס

KARPAS

BLESSING OVER A GREEN VEGETABLE

יַחַץ

YACHATZ

BREAKING THE MIDDLE MATZAH

מַגִּיד

MAGID

TELLING THE STORY OF THE EXODUS

*The Four Questions, the Four Children,
the Passover Story, the Ten Plagues, Dayeinu,
Passover Symbols, Watch-Night of the Eternal,
Hallel, and the Second Cup of Wine*

רָחְצָה

ROCHTZAH

WASHING THE HANDS BEFORE THE MEAL

♪ *The "Order of the Seder" is also a song that is sometimes sung in Hebrew at the beginning of a seder.*

מוֹצִיא/מַצָּה
MOTZI/MATZAH
BLESSING OVER THE MATZAH

מָרוֹר
MAROR
BLESSING OVER THE BITTER HERBS

כּוֹרֵךְ
KOREICH
EATING THE HILLEL SANDWICH

שֻׁלְחָן עוֹרֵךְ
SHULCHAN OREICH
THE MEAL IS SERVED

צָפוּן
TZAFUN
THE *AFIKOMAN* IS FOUND AND EATEN

בָּרֵךְ
BAREICH
BLESSING AFTER THE MEAL
Blessing, the Third Cup of Wine,
and Opening the Door for Elijah

הַלֵּל
HALLEL
POEMS AND SONGS OF PRAISE

נִרְצָה
NIRTZAH
CONCLUDING THE SEDER
Fourth Cup of Wine and Songs

The Seder

BEGINNING OUR SEDER

♫ *Some families begin the seder with a song. Parody or "piggyback" songs are frequent choices. Two examples of these songs may be found in the appendix on page 85. You can also begin with a* niggun, *a wordless melody.*

Why Do We Celebrate Passover?

READER: We gather tonight to celebrate the liberation of the Jewish people from slavery in Egypt more than three thousand years ago. Our ceremony is the seder, a Hebrew word that means "order." We read from the Haggadah, which means "the telling." We tell the story of our deliverance from Egypt using symbols, whose meaning we explore. These symbols are on our seder table and on our seder plate.

READER: Jewish tradition requires that each of us act as if we had personally gone forth from Egypt. Every generation is encouraged to make the story of the Exodus their own. In accordance with this obligation, each year our seder combines rituals and prayers developed over the millennia with contemporary readings and new practices for our joyous celebration.

READER: By telling the story of freedom on Passover (in Hebrew: *Pesach*), we celebrate our Jewish history. The story of the Exodus, however, is not just a Jewish story. It is a story that embodies humanity's passion for justice and freedom. Tonight, we celebrate the efforts of all people everywhere to free themselves, and others, from oppression. Our festive celebration is intended to be a source of inspiration and strength, to be drawn upon by each of us throughout the year as we strive to enhance our vigilance against injustice. It is our prayer that we may be inspired to take the steps necessary to free ourselves from the forces that limit hope and freedom.

READER: Throughout the world, families gather tonight and invite friends and neighbors of all religious beliefs (and those who may be alone or unable to make their own seder) to celebrate with them. Tonight we will learn together. We will discuss the Passover symbols, answer the Four Questions, sing songs, play games, give thanks, offer blessings, and remind one another that each of us came forth out of Egypt. We shall also

eat a meal worthy of royalty and drink four cups of wine. Why four cups of wine? According to one legend, we drink four cups of wine because royalty drank three cups of wine with their meals, and we are to outdo even kings and queens in our continuing quest for freedom.

READER: With grateful thanks, we welcome everyone to our Passover seder. Tonight, we shall fulfill once again the Torah's instruction to remember the story of the Exodus from Egypt all the days of our lives. Whether we have many Passover memories or are experiencing our first seder tonight, we joyously tell the story of the Exodus as one community.

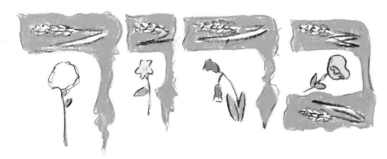

READER: Let us welcome each other as if it is our first Passover celebration with the traditional words of welcome to the seder table:

"Blessed are you who come."

Let us say together in Hebrew to all women at the seder table:

Together or repeat after the Reader:

בְּרוּכָה הַבָּאָה.

B'ruchah habaah.

Let us say together in Hebrew to all men at the seder table:

Together or repeat after the Reader:

בָּרוּךְ הַבָּא.

Baruch haba.

Hineih Mah Tov: **A Song of Harmony**

READER: "How good and pleasant it is when people live together in harmony" (Psalm 133:1).

May these words be a blessing for all who have come to our seder table tonight. As we begin, let us say in Hebrew these words from Psalm 133 and then join in singing *Hineih Mah Tov* (הִנֵּה מַה־טּוֹב).

Together or repeat after the Reader:

הִנֵּה מַה־טּוֹב וּמַה־נָּעִים שֶׁבֶת אַחִים גַּם יָחַד.

Hineih mah tov umah na-im shevet achim gam yachad.

How good and pleasant it is
when people live together in harmony.

♫ הִנֵּה מַה־טּוֹב *HINEIH MAH TOV*

Song leader:

הִנֵּה מַה־טּוֹב וּמַה־נָּעִים *Hineih mah tov umah na-im*
שֶׁבֶת אַחִים גַּם־יָחַד. *Shevet achim gam yachad.*

Together:

הִנֵּה מַה־טּוֹב וּמַה־נָּעִים *Hineih mah tov umah na-im*
שֶׁבֶת אַחִים גַּם־יָחַד. *Shevet achim gam yachad.*

Song leader:

הִנֵּה מַה־טּוֹב *Hineih mah tov*
שֶׁבֶת אַחִים גַּם־יָחַד. *Shevet achim gam yachad.*

Together:

הִנֵּה מַה־טּוֹב *Hineih mah tov*
שֶׁבֶת אַחִים גַּם־יָחַד. *Shevet achim gam yachad.*

Read or sung together:

♫ As we travel along the path of our lives
It's the people we meet who can change us.
If we are willing to seek, truly open our eyes
We'll find the song within that binds
Us . . . together.
(*Hineih Mah Tov,* by Sue Horowitz)

Blessing over the Festival Candles

READER: The lighting of candles in our home symbolizes lighting the lamps of our people—the spreading of light, joy, and the knowledge of God's ways. We light and bless the Festival candles tonight, marking the joy that Passover brings into our home.

בָּרוּךְ אַתָּה, יְיָ אֱלֹהֵינוּ, מֶלֶךְ הָעוֹלָם,
אֲשֶׁר קִדְּשָׁנוּ, בְּמִצְוֹתָיו וְצִוָּנוּ, לְהַדְלִיק
נֵר שֶׁל (שַׁבָּת וְשֶׁל) יוֹם טוֹב.

Baruch atah, Adonai Eloheinu, Melech haolam,
asher kid'shanu, b'mitzvotav v'tzivanu, l'hadlik
ner shel (Shabbat v'shel) Yom Tov.

Blessed are You, Eternal our God, Sovereign of the universe,
who sanctifies us with Your commandments and has
commanded us to kindle the (Sabbath and) Festival lights.

Blessing for Children

READER: On Shabbat (the Sabbath) and other Festivals and holidays, children are traditionally blessed by their parents or another loving adult. On Passover, we bless all children and children of all ages with the "Priestly Benediction" (Numbers 6:24–26). It is our prayer that all children may soon be blessed with love, freedom, and peace.

The Reader may proceed directly to the Priestly Benediction. Parents or those who wish to bless a child or children individually may do so at this time.

BLESSING FOR SONS

Adults may raise their hands above the heads of the sons.

יְשִׂמְךָ אֱלֹהִים כְּאֶפְרֵים וְכִמְנַשֶּׁה.

Y'simcha Elohim k'Efrayim v'chiM'nasheh.

May God bless you with the strength and
faithfulness of Ephraim and the wisdom of Manasseh.
(Based on Genesis 48:20)

Blessing for Daughters

Adults may raise their hands above the heads of the daughters.

יְשִׂימֵךְ אֱלֹהִים כְּשָׂרָה, כְּרִבְקָה, כְּרָחֵל, וּכְלֵאָה.

Y'simeich Elohim k'Sarah, k'Rivkah, k'Rachel, uch'Leah.

May God bless you with the strength and vision of Sarah,
with the wisdom and foresight of Rebecca, with the courage
and compassion of Rachel, and with the gentleness and
graciousness of Leah. (Based on Ruth 4:11)

Blessing for All Children: The "Priestly Benediction"

The Reader rises to offer the Priestly Benediction.

The Reader may recite the Hebrew, with adults joining together in the reading of the English, or the blessing may be read in unison in English. When reciting this blessing, the Reader may symbolically raise his/her hands above the heads of those being blessed.

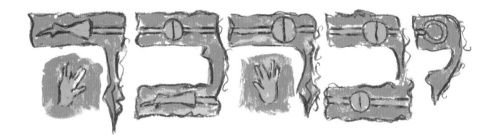

יְבָרֶכְךָ יְיָ וְיִשְׁמְרֶךָ.

Y'varech'cha Adonai v'yishm'recha.

May God bless you and keep you.

יָאֵר יְיָ פָּנָיו אֵלֶיךָ וִיחֻנֶּךָ.

Ya-eir Adonai panav eilecha vichuneka.

May God's light shine upon you,
and may God be gracious to you.

יִשָּׂא יְיָ פָּנָיו אֵלֶיךָ, וְיָשֵׂם לְךָ שָׁלוֹם.

Yisa Adonai panav eilecha, v'yaseim l'cha shalom.

May God's Presence be within you always,
and may you find peace.

THE SEDER SERVICE
BEFORE THE MEAL

Kiddush: **Blessing for the First Cup of Wine**

The Shehecheyanu *prayer immediately follows the blessing for the first cup of wine, without interruption.*

For children and those who do not drink wine, grape juice is an acceptable substitute.

READER: The *Kiddush* cup that holds the wine is our symbol of joy. The wine poured into the cup is our hope for life's sweetness. Together, poured to the brim, the cup reminds us of the fullness of our days.

During the seder, we will drink four cups of wine. Each cup symbolizes a different aspect of Passover. With the first cup, we remember God's promise to our ancestors and to every generation:

"I will free you from the labors of the Egyptians." (Exodus 6:6)

וְהוֹצֵאתִי אֶתְכֶם מִתַּחַת סִבְלֹת מִצְרַיִם.

V'hotzeiti etchem mitachat sivlot Mitzrayim.

As we drink, we celebrate this promise of freedom from slavery and oppression. From our enslavement in Egypt, we learn that there are times when bitterness is a companion to life's sweetness. The story of our deliverance teaches us that a life touched by God's Presence strengthens hope, providing us with the will to overcome the bitter and to rejoice in the sweetness and sanctity of every life.

The *Shehecheyanu* (שֶׁהֶחֱיָנוּ) is a prayer of gratitude recited at the beginning of special times. We recite it immediately after the blessing for the first cup of wine to give thanks for our opportunity to celebrate this holiday season together.

21

The Blessing

For the extended Festival Kiddush, *turn to page 86.*

The Reader raises his/her cup of wine.

READER: With song and praise, and with the symbols of Passover, let us renew the memories of our past. In love God has given us solemn days of joy and this Festival season of Passover, a remembrance of our departure from Egypt and a celebration of freedom and life.

On Shabbat, add the following text:

> Let us praise God with this symbol of joy and give thanks for the blessings of the past year; for life, health, and strength; for home, love, and friendship; for the discipline of our trials and temptations; for the happiness that has come to us out of our labors. You have ennobled us, O God, by the blessings of work and in love have sanctified us by the blessings of rest, through the commandment, "Six days you shall labor and do all your work, but the seventh day is a Sabbath of Adonai your God" (Exodus 20:9–10).

READER: Together let us raise the first cup of wine and say:

The blessing may be read or chanted in unison or by the Reader. The Reader may also read the blessing in Hebrew, one phrase at a time, with everyone joining in unison after each phrase and in the English, and then the blessing may be chanted.

בָּרוּךְ אַתָּה, יְיָ אֱלֹהֵינוּ, מֶלֶךְ הָעוֹלָם, בּוֹרֵא פְּרִי הַגָּפֶן.

*Baruch atah, Adonai Eloheinu, Melech haolam,
borei p'ri hagafen.*

Blessed are You, Eternal our God, Sovereign of the universe,
Creator of the fruit of the vine.

When the seder falls on a Saturday night, add the blessings (for Havdalah) found on page 88.

קַדֵּשׁ
Kadeish
First Cup of Wine

וּרְחַץ
Urchatz
Washing Hands

כַּרְפַּס
Karpas
Green Vegetable

יַחַץ
Yachatz
Middle Matzah

מַגִּיד
Magid
Telling the Story

רָחְצָה
Rochtzah
Washing Hands
before the Meal

מוֹצִיא/מַצָּה
Motzi/Matzah
Matzah

מָרוֹר
Maror
Bitter Herbs

כּוֹרֵךְ
Koreich
Hillel Sandwich

שֻׁלְחָן עוֹרֵךְ
Shulchan Oreich
The Meal Is Served

Shehecheyanu: A Prayer to Give Thanks

בָּרוּךְ אַתָּה, יְיָ אֱלֹהֵינוּ, מֶלֶךְ הָעוֹלָם,
שֶׁהֶחֱיָנוּ וְקִיְּמָנוּ וְהִגִּיעָנוּ לַזְּמַן הַזֶּה.

*Baruch atah, Adonai Eloheinu, Melech haolam,
shehecheyanu v'kiy'manu, v'higianu laz'man hazeh.*

Blessed are You, Eternal our God, Sovereign of the universe,
for giving us life, sustaining us,
and for enabling us to reach this season.

Drink the first cup of wine and refill the wine cups.

Ritual Washing of the Hands

READER: The washing of hands is a ritual of purification. We symbolically wash away the thoughts of our daily activities and any remnants of the slave mentality created by the many years of servitude our ancestors endured in Egypt. Later in our seder, we wash our hands again and say a blessing as we prepare to eat our festive meal.

The Reader pours water (from a "washing cup" into a bowl) over each hand, and then repeats the procedure, symbolically washing the hands for all those at the seder table.

As we tell the story of Passover, we reflect on the role of water in our quest to achieve freedom—in saving the life of Moses, in the parting of the Red Sea, and for quenching our thirst and renewing our spirit through our journey in the desert.

Passover Symbols

Hold up each symbol as its name is read.

READER: The symbols of Passover are represented on our table and our seder plate. On our seder plate we have a green vegetable (*karpas/*

קַדֵּשׁ
Kadeish
First Cup of Wine

וּרְחַץ
Urchatz
Washing Hands

כַּרְפַּס
Karpas
Green Vegetable

יַחַץ
Yachatz
Middle Matzah

מַגִּיד
Magid
Telling the Story

רָחְצָה
Rochtzah
Washing Hands
before the Meal

מוֹצִיא/מַצָּה
Motzi/Matzah
Matzah

מָרוֹר
Maror
Bitter Herbs

כּוֹרֵךְ
Koreich
Hillel Sandwich

שֻׁלְחָן עוֹרֵךְ
Shulchan Oreich
The Meal Is Served

"Red Sea" is a name that has historically been used in Haggadot to refer to the Sea of Reeds.

כַּרְפַּס), bitter herbs (*maror*/מָרוֹר), a roasted shank bone (*z'roa*/זְרוֹעַ), a roasted egg (*beitzah*/בֵּיצָה), and a sweet condiment (*charoset*/חֲרֹסֶת). As we tell the story of our deliverance from Egypt, we shall explore the meaning of each of these symbols as well as the significance of matzah (unleavened bread), Miriam's cup, and the cup of Elijah, which are on our seder table.

Karpas: Blessing for the Fruit of the Earth

Hold up the karpas.

READER: Tonight we praise God once again for creating the fruit of the earth, symbolized by the *karpas* (green vegetable) on our table. The first growth of spring, *karpas* represents rebirth and renewal. In the spirit of Passover, before we eat it we dip the *karpas* in salt water. We do so to remind ourselves of the tears shed by our ancestors while enslaved in Egypt.

The karpas *is distributed, and each person dips it in salt water.*

THE BLESSING

The blessing may be read or chanted in unison or by the Reader. The Reader may also read the blessing in Hebrew, one phrase at a time, with everyone joining in unison after each phrase and in the English, and then the blessing may be chanted.

בָּרוּךְ אַתָּה, יְיָ אֱלֹהֵינוּ, מֶלֶךְ הָעוֹלָם, ♫
בּוֹרֵא פְּרִי הָאֲדָמָה.

Baruch atah, Adonai Eloheinu, Melech haolam,
borei p'ri haadamah.

Blessed are You, Eternal our God, Sovereign of the universe,
Creator of the fruit of the earth.

Eat the karpas.

קַדֵּשׁ
Kadeish
First Cup of Wine

וּרְחַץ
Urchatz
Washing Hands

כַּרְפַּס
Karpas
Green Vegetable

יַחַץ
Yachatz
Middle Matzah

מַגִּיד
Magid
Telling the Story

רָחְצָה
Rochtzah
Washing Hands
before the Meal

מוֹצִיא/מַצָּה
Motzi/Matzah
Matzah

מָרוֹר
Marar
Bitter Herbs

כּוֹרֵךְ
Koreich
Hillel Sandwich

שֻׁלְחָן עוֹרֵךְ
Shulchan Oreich
The Meal Is Served

The Seder Service
before the Meal

Beitzah: The Roasted Egg

Hold up the roasted egg.

READER: Even before the Exodus from Egypt, Jews celebrated the creation of life each spring. The egg, like parsley, symbolizes the beginning and renewal of life. Round, without beginning or end, it also represents the cycles of the year and the cycles of life.

Matzah: Our Bread of Affliction

READER: We have on a plate on our table three pieces of matzah. Matzah is unleavened bread, bread that has not had time to rise, or leaven. It is the food we ate during our Exodus from Egypt. As the Torah teaches, "They baked unleavened cakes of the dough that they had taken out of Egypt, for it was not leavened, since they had been driven out of Egypt and could not delay" (Exodus 12:39).

The three pieces of matzah are a reminder to us of God's covenant with the Patriarchs and Matriarchs of the Jewish people—Abraham, Isaac, and Jacob and Sarah, Rebecca, Rachel, and Leah.

Before our meal, we shall give thanks to God for bringing forth bread from the earth and shall break and eat the upper matzah. As a reminder of our dual obligation to never forget the bitterness of slavery and to keep alive the hope of freedom, we shall break and eat the bottom matzah with *maror*, a bitter herb, and *charoset*, a sweet condiment that recalls the mortar our ancestors used for building Egyptian monuments.

The *Afikoman:* Breaking the Middle Matzah

READER: We now break the middle matzah in half. The larger piece is called the *afikoman*. It is our tradition to hide the *afikoman*. After the meal the young people at the seder table hunt for it and return it, possibly for a reward, so that the seder may be completed. The search for the *afikoman* reminds us that it is the memory of freedoms that have been lost that inspires each generation to continue the pursuit of liberty, tolerance, and justice.

The Reader holds up the afikoman. *Each person holds up a piece of matzah.*

TOGETHER:

> This is the bread of affliction that our ancestors ate in the land of Egypt. All who are hungry, let them come and eat. All who are in need, let them come celebrate Passover with

us. May it be God's will to redeem us from all trouble and all servitude. Next year at this season, may the whole house of Israel (and all peoples) be free!

♫ הָא לַחְמָא עַנְיָא דִי אֲכָלוּ אֲבָהָתָנָא בְּאַרְעָא דְמִצְרָיִם.
כָּל־דִּכְפִין יֵיתֵי וְיֵכֻל. כָּל־דִצְרִיךְ יֵיתֵי וְיִפְסַח. הָשַׁתָּא הָכָא.
לְשָׁנָה הַבָּאָה בְּאַרְעָא דְיִשְׂרָאֵל. הָשַׁתָּא עַבְדֵי,
לְשָׁנָה הַבָּאָה בְּנֵי חוֹרִין.

Return the matzot *to the seder table. The* afikoman *is hidden.*

A Symbol of Hope and the Responsibilities of Freedom

Raise the second half of the middle matzah.

READER: To our plate that held three pieces of matzah, we now return the second half of the middle matzah. For the oppressed, it is a symbol of hope. For free persons, it is a symbol of the responsibilities of freedom.

The story of the Exodus has brought hope to many peoples as they faced their own struggle for freedom. Dr. Martin Luther King Jr. (1929–1968), in the speeches, rallies, and marches of the American civil rights movement, explicitly invoked the story of the Exodus:

> (The Exodus) is something of the story of every people struggling for freedom. It is the first story of man's explicit quest for freedom. And it demonstrates the stages that seem to inevitably follow the quest for freedom.

This is the power of the story of the Exodus: it is both a historical story and a contemporary symbol of hope.

READER: Having washed away the remnants of slave mentality, we acknowledge that, blessed with freedom, we have responsibilities as free persons. As articulated by the great twentieth-century philosopher Rabbi Abraham Joshua Heschel:

> Freedom means more than mere emancipation. . . . Freedom presupposes the capacity for sacrifice. . . . The glory of a free society lies not only in the consciousness of my right to be free, and in my capacity to be free, but also in the realization of my fellow man's right to be free, and his capacity to be free. The issue we face is how to save man's belief in his capacity to be free.

An opportunity for a short discussion: Who are those struggling for freedom today? What are the responsibilities of free persons?

READER: May the story of the Exodus continue to be a source of hope for all those who seek freedom from persecution and

קַדֵּשׁ
Kadeish
First Cup of Wine

וּרְחַץ
Urchatz
Washing Hands

כַּרְפַּס
Karpas
Green Vegetable

יַחַץ
Yachatz
Middle Matzah

מַגִּיד
Magid
Telling the Story

רָחְצָה
Rochtzah
Washing Hands
before the Meal

מוֹצִיא/מַצָּה
Motzi/Matzah
Matzah

מָרוֹר
Maror
Bitter Herbs

כּוֹרֵךְ
Koreich
Hillel Sandwich

שֻׁלְחָן עוֹרֵךְ
Shulchan Oreich
The Meal Is Served

oppression and be a reminder to those who are the beneficiaries of freedom's blessings of the responsibilities they shoulder as free persons.

TOGETHER: Tonight we recite again the story of the Exodus and give thanks to God for delivering us from slavery to freedom. As family, friends, and neighbors, we, the beneficiaries of God's compassion, affirm our obligation to join with God and partner with one another to perform *tikkun olam*—doing our part to help repair the world. As free persons, we break the middle matzah into small pieces as a reminder of our responsibilities in a world that is still broken.

The Reader breaks the second half of the middle matzah into small pieces.

Let Us Remember: The Holocaust

READER: Let us remember the Holocaust (in Hebrew: the Shoah), the dark days and nights of Adolf Hitler and Nazi Germany (1933–1945), when men, women, and children across Europe were murdered solely because they were Jewish. We also remember the many others who were killed because of their ethnic origins, sexual orientation, disabilities, or political beliefs.

READER: We are obligated each year to participate in a seder and to eat matzah instead of bread during Passover. In 1944, the Jewish prisoners in the Nazi concentration camp at Bergen-Belsen desired to observe Passover. Enslaved at the concentration camp, they had little food and no matzah. Unsure what to do, the prisoners at Bergen-Belsen looked to their rabbis and teachers, imprisoned with them. These sages permitted the eating of leavened bread as a necessity of survival. This benediction was composed and recited on Passover:

An opportunity for a short discussion: Elie Wiesel, a Holocaust survivor, author and recipient of the Nobel Peace Prize, spoke about his memories of being liberated from Buchenwald when visiting the concentration camp in 2009:

"Memory has become a sacred duty of all people of good will. . . . When I was liberated (from Buchenwald) in 1945 . . . paradoxically, I was so hopeful then. Many of us were, although we had the right to give up on humanity, to give up on culture, to give up on education, to give up on the possibility of living one's life with dignity in a world that has no place for dignity. We rejected that possibility and we said, no, we must continue believing in the future."

Our God in heaven, behold it is evident and known to You that it is our desire to do Your will and to celebrate the Festival of Passover by eating matzah and by observing the prohibition of leavened food. But our heart is pained that the enslavement prevents us and we are in danger of our lives. Behold, we are prepared and are ready to fulfill the commandment: "And you shall live by them and not die by them."

Our prayer to You is that You may keep us alive and preserve us and redeem us speedily so that we may observe Your commandments and do Your will and serve You with a perfect heart. Amen.

Let us remember the Holocaust as we recite together names of concentration camps and ghettos where Jews perished:

Repeat after the Reader or together:

AUSCHWITZ · BELZEC · MAIDANEK · TREBLINKA

BUCHENWALD · THERESIENSTADT (TEREZIN) · VILNA · DACHAU

BERGEN-BELSEN · LVOV · WARSAW (PASSOVER 1943)

READER: Let us remember the sacrifice and the heroism of all men, women, and children who perished in the Holocaust.

TOGETHER: Let us remember their agony and their faith!

READER: Let us be true to their memory by being vigilant in the cause of freedom.

TOGETHER: Let us be true to their memory by being vigilant against indifference to persecution and injustice—at home and throughout the world!

READER: May our Exodus from Egypt and the memory of the Holocaust continue to strengthen our belief in God and our resolve to improve the human condition.

The Four Questions

READER: At our Passover seder, we ask four questions as we inquire:

"Why is this night different from all other nights?"

The questions ask why there is a change in our everyday routine for our Passover evening meal. By asking and answering these questions, we explore the meaning of Passover for our children and for all those at our seder table: for those who are unacquainted with the Passover symbols and rituals and for those who seek a deeper understanding of the story of the Exodus.

The youngest person at the seder table traditionally has the honor of being the first person to ask the Four Questions, followed by any children who also wish to participate. After the Four Questions have been asked, anyone at the seder table may add questions for us to explore as we tell the story of the Exodus and learn more about our people's passion for justice and freedom.

קַדֵּשׁ
Kadeish
First Cup of Wine

וּרְחַץ
Urchatz
Washing Hands

כַּרְפַּס
Karpas
Green Vegetable

יַחַץ
Yachatz
Middle Matzah

מַגִּיד
Magid
Telling the Story

רָחְצָה
Rochtzah
Washing Hands
before the Meal

מוֹצִיא/מַצָּה
Motzi/Matzah
Matzah

מָרוֹר
Maror
Bitter Herbs

כּוֹרֵךְ
Koreich
Hillel Sandwich

שֻׁלְחָן עוֹרֵךְ
Shulchan Oreich
The Meal Is Served

THE QUESTIONS

The Four Questions are asked. The questions may be read or chanted in English and/or in Hebrew.

מַה־נִּשְׁתַּנָּה הַלַּיְלָה הַזֶּה מִכָּל־הַלֵּילוֹת?

Mah nishtanah halailah hazeh mikol haleilot?

Why is this night different from all other nights?

FIRST QUESTION

שֶׁבְּכָל־הַלֵּילוֹת, אָנוּ אוֹכְלִין חָמֵץ וּמַצָּה;
הַלַּיְלָה הַזֶּה, כֻּלּוֹ מַצָּה.

*Sheb'chol haleilot, anu ochlin
chameitz umatzah;
halailah hazeh, kulo matzah?*

On all other nights we eat either
bread or matzah.
Why, on this night, do we eat only matzah?

SECOND QUESTION

שֶׁבְּכָל־הַלֵּילוֹת, אָנוּ אוֹכְלִין שְׁאָר יְרָקוֹת;
הַלַּיְלָה הַזֶּה, מָרוֹר.

*Sheb'chol haleilot, anu ochlin sh'ar y'rakot;
halailah hazeh, maror?*

On all other nights, we eat all kinds of herbs.
Why, on this night,
do we eat especially bitter herbs?

THIRD QUESTION

שֶׁבְּכָל־הַלֵּילוֹת, אֵין אָנוּ מַטְבִּילִין
אֲפִלּוּ פַּעַם אֶחָת;
הַלַּיְלָה הַזֶּה, שְׁתֵּי פְעָמִים.

*Sheb'chol haleilot, ein anu matbilin
afilu paam echat;
halailah hazeh, sh'tei f'amim?*

On all other nights, we do not dip herbs in any condiment.
Why, on this night, do we dip them twice?

קַדֵּשׁ
Kadeish
First Cup of Wine

וּרְחַץ
Urchatz
Washing Hands

כַּרְפַּס
Karpas
Green Vegetable

יַחַץ
Yachatz
Middle Matzah

מַגִּיד
Magid
Telling the Story

רָחְצָה
Rochtzah
Washing Hands
before the Meal

מוֹצִיא/מַצָּה
Motzi/Matzah
Matzah

מָרוֹר
Maror
Bitter Herbs

כּוֹרֵךְ
Koreich
Hillel Sandwich

שֻׁלְחָן עוֹרֵךְ
Shulchan Oreich
The Meal Is Served

FOURTH QUESTION

שֶׁבְּכָל־הַלֵּילוֹת, אָנוּ אוֹכְלִין בֵּין יוֹשְׁבִין וּבֵין מְסֻבִּין;
הַלַּיְלָה הַזֶּה, כֻּלָּנוּ מְסֻבִּין.

Sheb'chol haleilot, anu ochlin bein yoshvin uvein m'subin;
halailah hazeh, kulanu m'subin?

On all other nights, we eat either sitting upright or reclining.
Why, on this night, do we recline?

READER: Are there additional questions that anyone would like to ask? Not all questions can be answered at our seder. The answer to some questions may require additional study. What matters tonight is that questions are asked.

Reply to the Four Questions

"WHY IS THIS NIGHT DIFFERENT FROM ALL OTHER NIGHTS?"

READER: We celebrate tonight because we were Pharaoh's slaves in Egypt, and God delivered us from bondage to freedom. Had our ancestors not been redeemed from Egyptian slavery, we, our children, and our children's children would have remained slaves. Even if all of us were wise and educated by our study of Torah, it would still be our responsibility each year to tell the story of our deliverance from Egypt. To dwell at length on the remembrance of our Exodus from Egypt on Passover is considered praiseworthy.

עֲבָדִים הָיִינוּ לְפַרְעֹה בְּמִצְרָיִם. וַיּוֹצִיאֵנוּ יְיָ
אֱלֹהֵינוּ מִשָּׁם בְּיָד חֲזָקָה וּבִזְרוֹעַ נְטוּיָה.

Avadim hayinu l'faroh b'Mitzrayim. Vayotzi-einu Adonai
Eloheinu misham b'yad chazakah uvizroa n'tuyah.

We were slaves to Pharaoh in Egypt, and the Eternal,
our God, freed us from Egypt with a mighty hand
and an outstretched arm.

WHY, ON THIS NIGHT, DO WE EAT ONLY MATZAH?

READER: Matzah symbolizes both slavery and freedom. Matzah is our "bread of affliction." It is a symbol of our rush to freedom, the food we ate when liberated from Egyptian bondage. When our ancestors rushed to leave Egypt, they did not have time to wait for their bread to leaven. During Passover we eat matzah to remind us of our enslavement in Egypt and of the divine help we received during our Exodus.

קַדֵּשׁ
Kadeish
First Cup of Wine

וּרְחַץ
Urchatz
Washing Hands

כַּרְפַּס
Karpas
Green Vegetable

יַחַץ
Yachatz
Middle Matzah

מַגִּיד
Magid
Telling the Story

רָחְצָה
Rochtzah
Washing Hands
before the Meal

מוֹצִיא/מַצָּה
Motzi/Matzah
Matzah

מָרוֹר
Maror
Bitter Herbs

כּוֹרֵךְ
Koreich
Hillel Sandwich

שֻׁלְחָן עוֹרֵךְ
Shulchan Oreich
The Meal Is Served

WHY, ON THIS NIGHT, DO WE EAT ESPECIALLY BITTER HERBS?

READER: Bitter herbs, *maror,* represent the bitterness of slavery. We eat bitter herbs, later in our seder ceremony, so that we will never forget the bitter taste of oppression.

WHY, ON THIS NIGHT, DO WE DIP HERBS TWICE?

READER: *Karpas* is a symbol of renewed hope and the promise of spring. We dip *karpas* in salt water as a reminder that our ancestors viewed the hope of renewal through the tears of slavery. Later in our seder, we shall combine *maror* and *charoset. Maror* is dipped or mixed with *charoset* to remind us that we withstood the bitterness of slavery because it was sweetened by the hope of freedom.

> An opportunity for a short discussion: What are other historical or current symbols of freedom?

WHY, ON THIS NIGHT, DO WE RECLINE WHEN WE EAT?

READER: A pillow on our chair is a symbol of freedom. Historically, slaves sat on hard benches or on the floor when they ate, forced to rush through their meal in order to return to work. For our ancestors, reclining on pillows or couches, eating at leisure, and engaging in conversation were symbols of freedom. Our pillows symbolize our ability to recline as free persons, declaring to the world that we will not be enslaved.

The Four Children

The Reader may select someone to read each question and response.

READER: According to tradition, there are four types of sons and daughters of Israel: the wise one (*chacham*/חָכָם), the wicked one (*rasha*/רָשָׁע), the simple one (*tam*/תָּם), and the one who is unable to inquire or does not know what questions to ask (*she-eino yodei-a lishol*/שֶׁאֵינוֹ יוֹדֵעַ לִשְׁאוֹל). By answering the questions of all of our children, we begin to fulfill our responsibility to pass to a new generation the story of God's mercy and might and our hope for the future.

THE WISE ONE

> The wise one asks: "What are the rulings, the laws, and the traditions that God has commanded to us?"
> (Deuteronomy 6:20).

חָכָם מַה הוּא אוֹמֵר: מָה הָעֵדֹת וְהַחֻקִּים
וְהַמִּשְׁפָּטִים אֲשֶׁר צִוָּה יְיָ אֱלֹהֵינוּ אֶתְכֶם?

*Chacham mah hu omeir: Mah ha-eidot v'hachukim
v'hamishpatim asher tzivah Adonai Eloheinu etchem?*

קַדֵּשׁ
Kadeish
First Cup of Wine

וּרְחַץ
Urchatz
Washing Hands

כַּרְפַּס
Karpas
Green Vegetable

יַחַץ
Yachatz
Middle Matzah

מַגִּיד
Magid
Telling the Story

רָחְצָה
Rochtzah
Washing Hands
before the Meal

מוֹצִיא/מַצָּה
Motzi/Matzah
Matzah

מָרוֹר
Maror
Bitter Herbs

כּוֹרֵךְ
Koreich
Hillel Sandwich

שֻׁלְחָן עוֹרֵךְ
Shulchan Oreich
The Meal Is Served

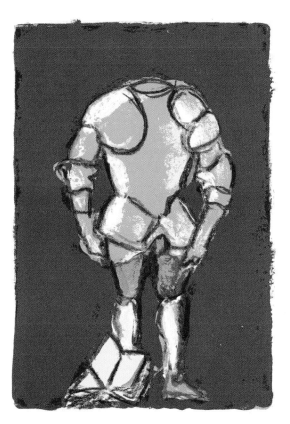

Our children are searching for wisdom and knowledge from the seder experience. It is our obligation to help them gain a deeper understanding of God's teachings through the story of the Exodus and strengthen their commitment to the pursuit of freedom, tolerance, and justice.

THE WICKED ONE

The wicked one inquires: "What is this service to you?"
(Exodus 12:26).

רָשָׁע מַה הוּא אוֹמֵר: מָה הָעֲבֹדָה הַזֹּאת לָכֶם?

Rasha mah hu omeir: Mah haavodah hazot lachem?

By saying "to you" and not "to us," our children are distancing themselves from their community. It is our obligation to make the seder a source for discovery of the spiritual foundation of Judaism to help them strengthen the bonds connecting them to their family and to their community.

THE SIMPLE ONE

The simple one asks: "What is this?" (Exodus 13:14).

תָּם מַה הוּא אוֹמֵר: מַה־זֹּאת?

Tam mah hu omeir: Mah zot?

Our children are seeking to better understand the story of the Exodus and the importance of the seder. It is our obligation to help make the seder an inspirational introduction to the study of the Jewish people's struggle for freedom through the generations.

THE ONE UNABLE TO ASK

For our sons and daughters who are unable to inquire or do not know what questions to ask, we begin: "You shall explain to your child on that day, 'It is because of what God did for me when I went free from Egypt.'" (Exodus 13:8).

וְשֶׁאֵינוֹ יוֹדֵעַ לִשְׁאוֹל,
וְשֶׁאֵינָה יוֹדַעַת לִשְׁאוֹל, אַתֶּם פִּתְחוּ לָהֶם.
שֶׁנֶּאֱמַר: וְהִגַּדְתָּ לְבִנְךָ בַּיּוֹם הַהוּא לֵאמֹר,
בַּעֲבוּר זֶה עָשָׂה יְיָ לִי בְּצֵאתִי מִמִּצְרָיִם.

V'she-eino yodei-a lishol,
v'she-eina yodaat lishol, atem pitchu lahem.
Shene-emar: V'higadta l'vincha bayom hahu leimor,
baavur zeh asah Adonai li b'tzeiti miMitzrayim.

It is our obligation to help our sons and daughters become involved in the joyful experience of the seder so that they may begin to feel a part of the Passover story of freedom and discover what questions they wish to ask.

קַדֵּשׁ
Kadeish
First Cup of Wine

וּרְחַץ
Urchatz
Washing Hands

כַּרְפַּס
Karpas
Green Vegetable

יַחַץ
Yachatz
Middle Matzah

מַגִּיד
Magid
Telling the Story

רָחְצָה
Rochtzah
Washing Hands
before the Meal

מוֹצִיא/מַצָּה
Motzi/Matzah
Matzah

מָרוֹר
Maror
Bitter Herbs

כּוֹרֵךְ
Koreich
Hillel Sandwich

שֻׁלְחָן עוֹרֵךְ
Shulchan Oreich
The Meal Is Served

READER: The one who is wise, wicked, simple, and does not know what questions to ask resides within each of us. By fulfilling our obligations for the seder, we learn more about ourselves and each other and make the story of Passover our own.

קַדֵּשׁ
Kadeish
First Cup of Wine

וּרְחַץ
Urchatz
Washing Hands

כַּרְפַּס
Karpas
Green Vegetable

יַחַץ
Yachatz
Middle Matzah

מַגִּיד
Magid
Telling the Story

רָחְצָה
Rachtzah
Washing Hands
before the Meal

מוֹצִיא/מַצָּה
Motzi/Matzah
Matzah

מָרוֹר
Maror
Bitter Herbs

כּוֹרֵךְ
Koreich
Hillel Sandwich

שֻׁלְחָן עוֹרֵךְ
Shulchan Oreich
The Meal Is Served

The Passover Story: God Our Guardian and Hope

The Reader raises his/her Kiddush *cup and recalls God's covenant with Abraham.*

Not in one country alone nor in one age alone have violent rulers risen against us. In every generation and in every land, tyrants have sought to destroy us. Ever since the covenant with Abraham, God has been our guardian and our hope.

שֶׁלֹּא אֶחָד בִּלְבָד עָמַד עָלֵינוּ לְכַלּוֹתֵנוּ.
אֶלָּא שֶׁבְּכָל־דּוֹר וָדוֹר עוֹמְדִים עָלֵינוּ לְכַלּוֹתֵנוּ.
וְהַקָּדוֹשׁ בָּרוּךְ הוּא מַצִּילֵנוּ מִיָּדָם.

TOGETHER: Whether we are celebrating our first seder or have celebrated a seder every year of our lives, whether we are young or old, it is well for all of us to consider the Passover story and how God has been our unfailing support through the millennia.

The Reader returns the Kiddush *cup to the table without drinking.*

♫   *V'HI SHE-AMDAH*

וְהִיא שֶׁעָמְדָה לַאֲבוֹתֵינוּ וְלָנוּ.
וְהִיא שֶׁעָמְדָה לַאֲבוֹתֵינוּ וְלָנוּ.
שֶׁלֹּא אֶחָד בִּלְבָד עָמַד עָלֵינוּ לְכַלּוֹתֵנוּ.
שֶׁלֹּא אֶחָד בִּלְבָד עָמַד עָלֵינוּ לְכַלּוֹתֵנוּ.
אֶלָּא שֶׁבְּכָל־דּוֹר וָדוֹר עוֹמְדִים עָלֵינוּ לְכַלּוֹתֵנוּ.
וְהַקָּדוֹשׁ בָּרוּךְ הוּא מַצִּילֵנוּ מִיָּדָם.

V'hi she-amdah laavoteinu v'lanu.
V'hi she-amdah laavoteinu v'lanu.
Shelo echad bilvad amad aleinu l'chaloteinu.
Shelo echad bilvad amad aleinu l'chaloteinu.
Eleh sheb'chol dor vador omdim aleinu l'chaloteinu.
V'hakadosh baruch hu matzileinu miyadam.

This is God's promise to our ancestors and to us:
Although one individual stands against us to destroy us,
another stands with us in difficult times.
In every generation, when some are blinded by hate,
others build bridges of understanding.
The Holy One, our Source of help, sustains us.

READER: The Passover story of deliverance and redemption that we now recount has provided a shared sense of experience to the Jewish people for three thousand years. Retold each year at our seder, the biblical story continues to sustain and enrich our collective spirit.

THE STORY OF JACOB, JOSEPH, AND EGYPTIAN SLAVERY

When there are young children at the seder table, they may be asked to tell the Passover story prior to the reading of the story of the Exodus.

READER: The Torah tells us that when harsh famine engulfed the land of Canaan, our forefather Jacob and his household went down into Egypt. Joseph, one of Jacob's sons, was already in Egypt. Joseph had helped Pharaoh eliminate the threat of famine during seven years of plentiful harvests. He was favored by Pharaoh, had risen high in the Egyptian court, and was able to provide possessions and security to his father and brothers. Jacob, Joseph, and their families, at first strangers in the land, came to feel at home in Egypt. After the famine was over in Canaan and it was possible to return to their homes, they remained—trusting that the memory of Joseph and their own contributions would keep them secure in Egypt.

TOGETHER: Joseph and all that generation died. And the generations of Jacob and Joseph were fruitful and had multiplied (Exodus 1:7). And a new Pharaoh arose over Egypt who did not know Joseph or the contributions that he and his household had made to Egyptian society over the generations (Exodus 1:8). And Pharaoh said: "The people of the children of Israel are too many and too mighty for us; come, let us deal wisely with them, lest it come to pass that when we are at war, they join themselves unto our enemies, and fight against us" (Exodus 1:10). Our ancestors were then forcibly enslaved. The Egyptians set over them taskmasters to afflict them with burdens and to build for Egyptian leaders royal cities and monuments.

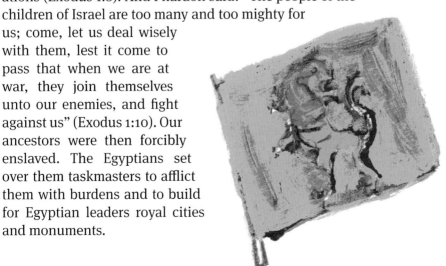

קַדֵּשׁ
Kadeish
First Cup of Wine

וּרְחַץ
Urchatz
Washing Hands

כַּרְפַּס
Karpas
Green Vegetable

יַחַץ
Yachatz
Middle Matzah

מַגִּיד
Magid
Telling the Story

רָחְצָה
Rochtzah
Washing Hands
before the Meal

מוֹצִיא/מַצָּה
Motzi/Matzah
Matzah

מָרוֹר
Maror
Bitter Herbs

כּוֹרֵךְ
Koreich
Hillel Sandwich

שֻׁלְחָן עוֹרֵךְ
Shulchan Oreich
The Meal Is
Served

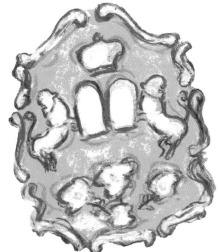

The Story of Moses and the Liberation from Egypt

READER: And so Pharaoh commanded the death of all sons born to our ancestors enslaved in Egypt. But Shiphrah and Puah, the midwives present at the births, refused to obey Pharaoh and did not distinguish between sons and daughters (Exodus 1:15–17). When one Israelite woman gave birth to a son, she hid him from the Egyptians. After he grew too old to hide, she put him in a basket and placed it among the reeds in the Nile. His older sister hid nearby to see what would happen to her brother. When Pharaoh's daughter came to bathe in the river, she found the baby in the basket. The baby's sister offered to find her an Israelite woman to nurse the baby. The woman she brought was the baby's own mother. When he grew older, his mother returned the baby to Pharaoh's daughter, who adopted him. She named him Moses, meaning "I drew him out of the water," and raised him in Pharaoh's court (Exodus 2:1–10).

TOGETHER: Moses was adopted by the Egyptian royal family and grew to manhood as a prince of Egypt. When he was grown, he saw an Egyptian taskmaster beating a Jewish slave. Moses killed the taskmaster and was forced to leave Egypt, fleeing to the land of Midian (Exodus 2:11–15). At an oasis, Moses came upon the daughters of Jethro, a Midianite priest, as they were drawing water from a well. Moses protected the women from a band of bullying shepherds. After the daughters told their father what happened, he invited Moses to their home and soon offered Zipporah, his oldest daughter, to Moses as a wife (Exodus 2:16–21).

READER: God heard the cries of our ancestors in bondage in Egypt (Exodus 2:23–24). One day while Moses was tending Jethro's flock, God appeared to Moses through a "burning bush," a bush that burned but miraculously was not consumed (Exodus 3:1–3). God commanded Moses to return to Egypt and to tell Pharaoh to free the Israelites from slavery and oppression (Exodus 3:7–4:17). On the journey, danger to Moses and his family was averted by the bravery and quick thinking of his wife Zipporah (Exodus 4:24–26).

TOGETHER: In Egypt, Moses spoke the word of God to Pharaoh, saying, "Let my people go!" (Exodus 5:1). When Pharaoh refused to release our ancestors from slavery, God afflicted the people and land of Egypt

קַדֵּשׁ
Kadeish
First Cup of Wine

וּרְחַץ
Ur'chatz
Washing Hands

כַּרְפַּס
Karpas
Green Vegetable

יַחַץ
Yachatz
Middle Matzah

מַגִּיד
Magid
Telling the Story

רָחְצָה
Rochtzah
Washing Hands
before the Meal

מוֹצִיא/מַצָּה
Matzi/Matzah
Matzah

מָרוֹר
Maror
Bitter Herbs

כּוֹרֵךְ
Koreich
Hillel Sandwich

שֻׁלְחָן עוֹרֵךְ
Shulchan Oreich
The Meal Is Served

with ten plagues, each one worse than the one before. It was only after the tenth plague, the slaying of the firstborn, that Pharaoh yielded and allowed us to begin our departure from Egypt.

READER: After his decision, Pharaoh had a change of heart and mobilized his army. As our ancestors approached the shores of the Red Sea seven days after our Exodus from Egypt, they saw the Egyptian army pursuing them and were filled with fear. Unless we were able to cross the sea, Pharaoh would destroy us. God, however, did not at first part the waters for our passage to dry land. The midrash (a commentary that explains biblical texts) teaches that it was only after one man, Nachshon ben Aminadav, acting with the courage of a free person and ready to take the ultimate risk for freedom, walked into the undivided waters of the Red Sea that God parted the waters (BT *Sotah* 37a; *B'midbar Rabbah* 13:7). When the Egyptians pursued us into the sea, God saved us by causing the sea to close in on the Egyptians, drowning them.

TOGETHER:

> And God brought us forth out of Egypt with a mighty hand
> and an outstretched arms and with signs and wonders.
> (Deuteronomy 26:8).

וַיּוֹצִאֵנוּ יְיָ מִמִּצְרַיִם בְּיָד חֲזָקָה וּבִזְרֹעַ נְטוּיָה וּבְמֹרָא
גָּדֹל וּבְאֹתוֹת וּבְמֹפְתִים.

And God commanded us to observe the Passover each year and to declare God's might and mercy to our children throughout all generations.

THE TEN PLAGUES

READER: Though our ancestors were redeemed from slavery and we have rejoiced to see the oppressors overcome, our joys and triumphs are diminished by the suffering of others. Even as God saved us, God taught us not to rejoice in the suffering of other people. As the sea closed over the pursuing Egyptians, God declared:

> "My creatures are drowning, and you are singing?"
> (BT *M'gillah* 10b)

An opportunity for a short discussion: What are the plagues we live with in our world today?

We now join together to recite each of the ten plagues while removing a drop of wine from our cups. With this act, we lessen our joy, symbolically acknowledging the suffering of the Egyptians, and envision ourselves casting out every plague that threatens our humanity.

קַדֵּשׁ
Kadeish
First Cup of Wine

וּרְחַץ
Urchatz
Washing Hands

כַּרְפַּס
Karpas
Green Vegetable

יַחַץ
Yachatz
Middle Matzah

מַגִּיד
Magid
Telling the Story

רָחְצָה
Rochtzah
Washing Hands
before the Meal

מוֹצִיא/מַצָּה
Motzi/Matzah
Matzah

מָרוֹר
Maror
Bitter Herbs

כּוֹרֵךְ
Koreich
Hillel Sandwich

שֻׁלְחָן עוֹרֵךְ
Shulchan Oreich
The Meal Is Served

קַדֵּשׁ
Kadeish
First Cup of Wine

וּרְחַץ
Urchatz
Washing Hands

כַּרְפַּס
Karpas
Green Vegetable

יַחַץ
Yachatz
Middle Matzah

מַגִּיד
Magid
Telling the Story

רָחְצָה
Rochtzah
Washing Hands
before the Meal

מוֹצִיא/מַצָּה
Motzi/Matzah
Matzah

מָרוֹר
Maror
Bitter Herbs

כּוֹרֵךְ
Koreich
Hillel Sandwich

שֻׁלְחָן עוֹרֵךְ
Shulchan Oreich
The Meal Is Served

Use a finger or spoon to remove wine from your cup and place it on a plate. Everyone at the seder table joins with the Reader to recite the plagues in Hebrew and/or English.

TOGETHER:

DAM · BLOOD · דָּם

TZ'FARDEI-A · FROGS · צְפַרְדֵּעַ

KINIM · LICE · כִּנִּים

AROV · WILD BEASTS · עָרוֹב

DEVER · BLIGHT · דֶּבֶר

SH'CHIN · BOILS · שְׁחִין

BARAD · HAIL · בָּרָד

ARBEH · LOCUSTS · אַרְבֶּה

CHOSHECH · DARKNESS · חֹשֶׁךְ

MAKAT B'CHOROT · SLAYING OF THE FIRSTBORN
מַכַּת בְּכוֹרוֹת

READER: After crossing the Red Sea, our ancestors celebrated with song, praising the omnipotence of God (Exodus 15:1–21). Tonight, we recite part of this Song of the Sea, giving thanks once again to God for our freedom and commemorating the splitting of the Red Sea.

Together or repeat after the Reader:

מִי כָמֹכָה   *MI CHAMOCHAH*   ♫

מִי כָמֹכָה בָּאֵלִם, יְיָ!   *Mi chamochah ba-eilim, Adonai!*
מִי כָּמֹכָה נֶאְדָּר בַּקֹּדֶשׁ,   *Mi kamochah nedar bakodesh,*
נוֹרָא תְהִלֹת עֹשֵׂה פֶלֶא!   *nora t'hilot oseih fele!*

יְיָ יִמְלֹךְ לְעוֹלָם וָעֶד.   *Adonai yimloch l'olam va-ed.*

SONG OF THE SEA

Who is like You, God, among the mighty!
Who is like You, majestic in holiness,
awesome in splendor, working wonders!

God will reign forever and ever.

Miriam's Cup

READER: According to a midrash, the prophet Miriam predicted the birth of her baby brother Moses (BT *M'gillah* 14a), guarded him as he floated down the Nile, witnessed Pharaoh's daughter drawing him out of the river, and arranged for their mother to care for the infant Moses. Celebrating their safe crossing of the Red Sea, Miriam led the women in joyous dancing (Exodus 15:20–21). According to the Rabbis, God honored Miriam's bravery and devotion to the Jewish people by giving her a well filled with water, which miraculously accompanied our ancestors throughout their journey in the desert (BT *Taanit* 9a). "Miriam's Well" quenched the thirst and renewed the spirit of our ancestors as they overcame the hardships of the Exodus.

Reader raises Miriam's cup.

We have placed on our seder table this cup of Miriam—*kos Miryam*. It is filled with water to honor Miriam's role ensuring our people's survival during our forty-year journey in the desert. We now each take a sip of water to remember this remarkable woman who was a prophet and a guardian of our people.

The leader takes a sip from the cup. The cup is passed around the table. Each person may drink from the cup, pour a little water from the cup into their cup and drink, or drink from their cup of water on the seder table.

Dayeinu: "It Would Have Been Sufficient"

READER: *Dayeinu* is a song of gratitude. *Dayeinu* means "It would have been sufficient" or "enough." As we rejoice in the many blessings bestowed upon us in the journey from slavery to freedom, we give thanks to God, acknowledging that even a single blessing "would have been sufficient." *Dayeinu* celebrates our relationship with God. The song is a reminder to each of us and a lesson to each new generation of the blessings we have received and our responsibility to ensure that all men, women, and children know the gifts of freedom.

Before we sing, we read each of the verses, concluding each verse by saying together in a loud, strong voice: *Dayeinu!*

Everyone at the seder table may take turns being the Reader. All join together to say, "Dayeinu!"

READER: How manifold are the blessings and favors that God has conferred upon us! Had God brought us out of Egypt, and not divided the Sea for us—*Dayeinu!*

READER: Had God divided the sea for us, and not sustained us for forty years in the desert—*Dayeinu!*

Kadeish
First Cup of Wine

וּרְחַץ
Ur'chatz
Washing Hands

כַּרְפַּס
Karpas
Green Vegetable

יַחַץ
Yachatz
Middle Matzah

מַגִּיד
Magid
Telling the Story

רָחְצָה
Rochtzah
Washing Hands
before the Meal

מוֹצִיא מַצָּה
Motzi Matzah
Matzah

מָרוֹר
Maror
Bitter Herbs

כּוֹרֵךְ
Koreich
Hillel Sandwich

The Seder Service
before the Meal

45

READER: Had God sustained us for forty years in the desert, and not fed us with manna—*Dayeinu!*

READER: Had God fed us with manna, and not ordained the Sabbath—*Dayeinu!*

READER: Had God ordained the Sabbath, and not drawn us close to Mount Sinai—*Dayeinu!*

READER: Had God drawn us close to Mount Sinai, and not given us the Torah—*Dayeinu!*

READER: Had God given us the Torah, and not brought us into the Land of Israel—*Dayeinu!*

READER: Had God brought us into the Land of Israel, and not sent us prophets of truth and justice—*Dayeinu!*

READER: Had God sent us prophets of truth and justice, and not given us the strength to keep alive hope through the generations—*Dayeinu!*

READER: Had God given us the strength to keep alive hope through the generations, and not given us the gift of the courage and compassion of the righteous men and women among us—*Dayeinu!*

Sung together in Hebrew to the traditional melody. All join in together or follow song leader in chorus.

דַּיֵּנוּ　　*DAYEINU* ♫

אִלּוּ הוֹצִיא, הוֹצִיאָנוּ	*Ilu hotzi, hotzianu*
הוֹצִיאָנוּ, מִמִּצְרַיִם	*Hotzianu, miMitzrayim*
הוֹצִיאָנוּ, מִמִּצְרַיִם	*Hotzianu, miMitzrayim*
דַּיֵּנוּ.	*Dayeinu!*

Chorus:

דַּיֵּנוּ, דַּיֵּנוּ, דַּיֵּנוּ	*Day-day-einu (repeat 3 times)*
דַּיֵּנוּ דַּיֵּנוּ	*Dayeinu dayeinu*

אִלּוּ נָתַן, נָתַן לָנוּ	*Ilu natan, natan lanu*
נָתַן לָנוּ אֶת־הַשַּׁבָּת	*Natan lanu et haShabbat*
נָתַן לָנוּ אֶת־הַשַּׁבָּת	*Natan lanu et haShabbat*
דַּיֵּנוּ.	*Dayeinu!*

Chorus:

דַּיֵּנוּ, דַּיֵּנוּ, דַּיֵּנוּ	*Day-day-einu (repeat 3 times)*
דַּיֵּנוּ דַּיֵּנוּ	*Dayeinu dayeinu*

קַדֵּשׁ
Kadeish
First Cup of Wine

וּרְחַץ
Urchatz
Washing Hands

כַּרְפַּס
Karpas
Green Vegetable

יַחַץ
Yachatz
Middle Matzah

מַגִּיד
Magid
Telling the Story

רָחְצָה
Rochtzah
Washing Hands before the Meal

מוֹצִיא/מַצָּה
Motzi/Matzah
Matzah

מָרוֹר
Maror
Bitter Herbs

כּוֹרֵךְ
Koreich
Hillel Sandwich

שֻׁלְחָן עוֹרֵךְ
Shulchan Oreich
The Meal Is Served

The Seder Service before the Meal

46

אִלּוּ נָתַן, נָתַן לָנוּ   *Ilu natan, natan lanu*

נָתַן לָנוּ אֶת־הַתּוֹרָה,   *Natan lanu et haTorah*

נָתַן לָנוּ אֶת־הַתּוֹרָה   *Natan lanu et haTorah*

דַּיֵּנוּ.   *Dayeinu!*

Chorus:

דַּיֵּנוּ, דַּיֵּנוּ, דַּיֵּנוּ   *Day-day-einu (repeat 3 times)*

דַּיֵּנוּ דַּיֵּנוּ   *Dayeinu dayeinu*

If we had been brought forth from Egypt,
Dayeinu!

If we had been given the Sabbath,
Dayeinu!

If we had been given the Torah,
Dayeinu!

Remembering the Exodus: Three Passover Symbols

Hold up each symbol as its name is read.

READER: Should enemies again rise against us, the remembrance of the Exodus from Egypt will never fail to inspire us with new courage and strengthen our faith in God, who redeems the oppressed. Exploring the meaning of the Passover symbols helps us to remember. Rabban Gamliel, one of Judaism's great scholars (first century CE), taught that whoever does not discuss or expound upon the symbolic meaning of the *"pesach"* (shank bone), "matzah," and *"maror"* (bitter herbs) has not truly celebrated the Passover Festival.

READER: What is the meaning of the *pesach?*

TOGETHER: The shank bone reminds us that God passed over our houses and spared us on the "Watch-Night" (Exodus 12:26–27). When Pharaoh refused to release us from slavery, God afflicted the people of Egypt with the tenth plague, the slaying of the firstborn. The doorposts of our houses were marked with lamb's blood so that God would pass over our homes, and our lives would be spared.

READER: As God has saved us from all kinds of distress, so may God always inspire us with courage to remove every trace of bondage among all peoples.

In the days of the ancient Temple in Jerusalem, our ancestors ate the Passover sacrifice of a lamb, the pesach, *as a remembrance that God passed over our houses. After the destruction of the Second Temple in 70 CE, the shank bone (z'roa) was substituted to symbolize the Passover sacrifice.*

READER: What is the meaning of *matzah?*

TOGETHER: Matzah is unleavened bread that symbolizes both slavery and freedom. It is our "bread of affliction," and a symbol of the divine help we received when we were liberated from Egyptian bondage (Exodus 12:39).

READER: As God has liberated us from Egyptian bondage, so may God always inspire us to help the afflicted.

READER: What is the meaning of *maror?*

TOGETHER: *Maror* is a bitter herb. It reminds us that the lives of our ancestors were made bitter from the oppression of Egyptian slavery (Exodus 1:14).

READER: As God has blessed us with freedom, so may God always inspire us to be messengers of God's word to those in need of hope.

The Watch-Night of the Eternal

READER: "You shall tell your child on that day: 'It is because of what God did for me when I came forth out from Egypt'" (Exodus 13:8).

This passage in the Book of Exodus is the inspiration for the most important words spoken during the Passover seder:

TOGETHER:

🎵 In every generation each individual is bound to regard himself or herself as if he or she had personally gone forth from Egypt.

בְּכָל־דּוֹר וָדוֹר חַיָּב אָדָם לִרְאוֹת אֶת־עַצְמוֹ כְּאִלּוּ
הוּא יָצָא מִמִּצְרָיִם.

*B'chol dor vador, chayav adam lirot et-atzmo k'ilu
hu yatza miMitzrayim.*

READER: The words we have spoken express the universal experiences we seek from our seder. It is not "each Jew" who must feel as if he or she came forth out of Egypt, but "each individual."

TOGETHER: "I" am bound, therefore, to live my life "as if" God redeemed me from persecution, oppression, and slavery. As a beneficiary of the miracles that God performed, I discuss the rituals and symbols of Passover to bring the events from the Exodus into my daily life.

קַדֵּשׁ
Kadeish
First Cup of Wine

וּרְחַץ
Urchatz
Washing Hands

כַּרְפַּס
Karpas
Green Vegetable

יַחַץ
Yachatz
Middle Matzah

מַגִּיד
Magid
Telling the Story

רָחְצָה
Rochtzah
Washing Hands
before the Meal

מוֹצִיא/מַצָּה
Motzi/Matzah
Matzah

מָרוֹר
Maror
Bitter Herbs

כּוֹרֵךְ
Koreich
Hillel Sandwich

שֻׁלְחָן עוֹרֵךְ
Shulchan Oreich
The Meal Is Served

"Watch-Night" refers to Exodus 12:42, which charges the children of Israel to observe a night of Passover through all generations.

The Seder Service before the Meal

51

READER: This is the power of our seder and the story of the Exodus: it is a shared Jewish experience that has historical and contemporary significance to persons of all faiths.

As we "leave Egypt" and carry the events of the Exodus into our daily lives, let us give thanks and offer praises to God for the miracles we have seen.

Raise cups of wine.

TOGETHER:

Therefore, we are bound to thank, praise, laud, glorify, extol, honor, bless, exalt, and revere the Eternal our God, who performed all these miracles for our mothers and fathers and for us. God brought us forth from slavery to freedom, from sorrow to joy, from mourning to festivity, and from servitude to redemption. Let us therefore sing a new song in God's presence. Hallelujah!

לְפִיכָךְ אֲנַחְנוּ חַיָּבִים לְהוֹדוֹת, לְהַלֵּל, לְשַׁבֵּחַ, לְפָאֵר,
לְרוֹמֵם, לְהַדֵּר, לְבָרֵךְ, לְעַלֵּה, וּלְקַלֵּס, לְמִי שֶׁעָשָׂה
לַאֲבוֹתֵינוּ וּלְאִמּוֹתֵינוּ וְלָנוּ אֶת־כָּל־הַנִּסִּים הָאֵלֶּה.
וְהוֹצִיאָנוּ מֵעַבְדוּת לְחֵרוּת, מִיָּגוֹן לְשִׂמְחָה, מֵאֵבֶל לְיוֹם
טוֹב. וּמֵאֲפֵלָה לְאוֹר גָּדוֹל. וּמִשִּׁעְבּוּד לִגְאֻלָּה. וְנֹאמַר
לְפָנָיו שִׁירָה חֲדָשָׁה. הַלְלוּיָהּ!

*L'fichach anachnu chayavim l'hodot, l'hallel, l'shabei-ach,
l'fa-eir, l'romeim, l'hadeir, l'vareich, l'aleih ul'kaleis, l'mi
she-asah laavoteinu ul'imoteinu v'lanu et kol hanisim ha-eileh.
V'hotzianu mei-avdut l'cheirut, miyagon l'simchah,
mei-eivel l'yom tov. Umei-afeilah l'or gadol. Umishibud ligulah.
V'nomar l'fanav shirah chadashah. Hal'luyah!*

Return the cups of wine, untasted, to the seder table.

Since we raise our cups of wine here to praise God and not to offer a blessing, after our tribute we return the cups to the table without drinking.

Hallel: **Songs of Praise**

READER: Our Rabbis teach that *Hallel*, psalms of gratitude and praise, were sung to God at the shores of the Red Sea. We sing God's praises now for redeeming us from persecution, oppression, and slavery and for the promise of freedom and peace for all peoples.

קַדֵּשׁ
Kadeish
First Cup of Wine

וּרְחַץ
Ur'chatz
Washing Hands

כַּרְפַּס
Karpas
Green Vegetable

יַחַץ
Yachatz
Middle Matzah

מַגִּיד
Magid
Telling the Story

רָחְצָה
Rochtzah
Washing Hands
before the Meal

מוֹצִיא/מַצָּה
Motzi/Matzah
Matzah

מָרוֹר
Maror
Bitter Herbs

כּוֹרֵךְ
Koreich
Hillel Sandwich

שֻׁלְחָן עוֹרֵךְ
Shulchan Oreich
The Meal Is Served

Read responsively, alternating between group and reader.

HALLEL: AN INTERPRETATION OF PSALM 113

Halleluyah.

O servants of God, give praise;
   praise the name of God.

*Let the name of God be blessed
   now and forever.*

From the rising of the sun to its going down
   the name of God is praised.

*God is exalted above all nations;
God's glory is above the heavens.*

Who is like the Eternal our God,
   who, enthroned on high,

*sees what is below,
in heaven and on earth?*

Who raises the poor from the dust,
   lifts up the needy from the ashes;

*to set them with the great,
with the greats of God's people. Halleluyah.*

HALLEL: AN INTERPRETATION OF PSALM 114

When Israel went forth from Egypt,
the house of Jacob from a people of strange speech;

*Judah became God's sanctuary,
   Israel, God's dominion.*

The sea saw them, and fled;
   the Jordan flowed backward.

*The mountains skipped like rams,
   hills like sheep.*

What frightened you, O sea, that you fled?
   Jordan, that you flowed backward,

*mountains that you skipped like rams,
   hills like sheep?*

Tremble, O earth, at the presence of God,
   at the presence of the God of Jacob,

*who turned the rock into a pool of water,
   the flinty rock into a fountain.*

קַדֵּשׁ
Kadeish
First Cup of Wine

וּרְחַץ
Urchatz
Washing Hands

כַּרְפַּס
Karpas
Green Vegetable

יַחַץ
Yachatz
Middle Matzah

מַגִּיד
Magid
Telling the Story

רָחְצָה
Rochtzah
Washing Hands
before the Meal

מוֹצִיא/מַצָּה
Motzi/Matzah
Matzah

מָרוֹר
Maror
Bitter Herbs

כּוֹרֵךְ
Koreich
Hillel Sandwich

שֻׁלְחָן עוֹרֵךְ
Shulchan Oreich
The Meal Is Served

The Seder Service
before the Meal

54

Blessing for the Second Cup of Wine

READER: Now we remember God's promise to our ancestors and to every generation:

"I will deliver you from their bondage." (Exodus 6:6)

וְהִצַּלְתִּי אֶתְכֶם מֵעֲבֹדָתָם.

V'hitzalti etchem mei-avodatam.

READER: We drink the second cup of wine to celebrate the survival of the Jewish people. We remember how, enslaved in Egypt, we retained our belief in God. Our faith and hope for the future gave us the will to survive and, ultimately, the strength to pursue the freedom promised by God.

TOGETHER: We remember all those men, women, and children who fought for freedom from oppression throughout our generations, from the days of the Exodus, the Spanish Inquisition, the Holocaust, and right up to the present day.

THE BLESSING

The blessing may be read or chanted in unison or by the Reader. The Reader also may read the blessing in Hebrew, one phrase at a time, with everyone joining in unison after each phrase and in the English, and then the blessing may be chanted.

READER: Together let us raise the second cup of wine and say:

בָּרוּךְ אַתָּה, יְיָ אֱלֹהֵינוּ, מֶלֶךְ הָעוֹלָם,
בּוֹרֵא פְּרִי הַגָּפֶן.

*Baruch atah, Adonai Eloheinu, Melech haolam,
borei p'ri hagafen.*

Blessed are You, Eternal our God, Sovereign of the universe,
who has created the fruit of the vine.

Drink the second cup of wine, and refill the wine cups.

קַדֵּשׁ
Kadeish
First Cup of Wine

וּרְחַץ
Urchatz
Washing Hands

כַּרְפַּס
Karpas
Green Vegetable

יַחַץ
Yachatz
Middle Matzah

מַגִּיד
Magid
Telling the Story

רָחְצָה
Rochtzah
Washing Hands
before the Meal

מוֹצִיא/מַצָּה
Motzi/Matzah
Matzah

מָרוֹר
Maror
Bitter Herbs

כּוֹרֵךְ
Koreich
Hillel Sandwich

שֻׁלְחָן עוֹרֵךְ
Shulchan Oreich
The Meal Is Served

Blessings for Washing of Hands and for Matzah

The blessings for matzah immediately follow the blessing for washing hands, without interruption.

The blessing may be read or chanted by the Reader, or in unison. The Reader may read the blessing in Hebrew, one phrase at a time, with everyone joining in unison after each phrase and in the English, and then the blessing may be chanted.

READER: When we began our seder, we had three pieces of matzah on a plate. We now break and distribute the upper matzah.

The upper matzah is broken, and a piece is distributed to all present.

READER: Before performing the *mitzvah* (commandment) of eating the Passover matzah and our Festival meal, we wash our hands and recite the blessings.

WASHING OF HANDS AND THE BLESSING

The Reader pours water (from a "washing cup" into a bowl) over each hand and then repeats the procedure, symbolically washing the hands for all those at the seder table. Those at the seder table may wash their hands or symbolically join with the Reader.

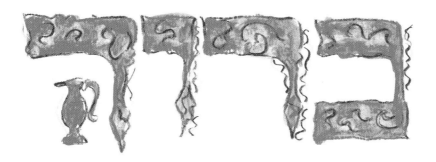

בָּרוּךְ אַתָּה, יְיָ אֱלֹהֵינוּ, מֶלֶךְ הָעוֹלָם,
אֲשֶׁר קִדְּשָׁנוּ, בְּמִצְוֹתָיו וְצִוָּנוּ, עַל נְטִילַת יָדָיִם.

*Baruch atah, Adonai Eloheinu, Melech haolam,
asher kid'shanu, b'mitzvotav v'tzivanu, al n'tilat yadayim.*

Blessed are You, Eternal our God, Sovereign of the universe,
who has sanctified us with Your commandments and
has commanded us concerning the washing of the hands.

קַדֵּשׁ
Kadeish
First Cup of Wine

וּרְחַץ
Urchatz
Washing Hands

כַּרְפַּס
Karpas
Green Vegetable

יַחַץ
Yachatz
Middle Matzah

מַגִּיד
Magid
Telling the Story

רָחְצָה
Rochtzah
Washing Hands
before the Meal

מוֹצִיא/מַצָּה
Motzi/Matzah
Matzah

מָרוֹר
Maror
Bitter Herbs

כּוֹרֵךְ
Koreich
Hillel Sandwich

שֻׁלְחָן עוֹרֵךְ
Shulchan Oreich
The Meal Is Served

Blessing over Matzah

קַדֵּשׁ
Kadeish
First Cup of Wine

וּרְחַץ
Urchatz
Washing Hands

כַּרְפַּס
Karpas
Green Vegetable

יַחַץ
Yachatz
Middle Matzah

מַגִּיד
Magid
Telling the Story

רָחְצָה
Rochtzah
Washing Hands
before the Meal

מוֹצִיא/מַצָּה
Motzi/Matzah
Matzah

מָרוֹר
Maror
Bitter Herbs

כּוֹרֵךְ
Koreich
Hillel Sandwich

שֻׁלְחָן עוֹרֵךְ
Shulchan Oreich
The Meal Is Served

בָּרוּךְ אַתָּה, יְיָ אֱלֹהֵינוּ, מֶלֶךְ הָעוֹלָם,
הַמּוֹצִיא לֶחֶם מִן הָאָרֶץ.

*Baruch atah, Adonai Eloheinu, Melech haolam,
hamotzi lechem min haaretz.*

Blessed are You, Eternal our God, Sovereign of the universe,
who brings forth bread from the earth.

בָּרוּךְ אַתָּה, יְיָ אֱלֹהֵינוּ, מֶלֶךְ הָעוֹלָם,
אֲשֶׁר קִדְּשָׁנוּ, בְּמִצְוֹתָיו וְצִוָּנוּ, עַל אֲכִילַת מַצָּה.

*Baruch atah, Adonai Eloheinu, Melech haolam,
asher kid'shanu, b'mitzvotav v'tzivanu, al achilat matzah.*

Blessed are You, Eternal our God, Sovereign of the universe,
who has sanctified us with Your commandments and has
commanded us concerning the eating of unleavened bread.

Eat the matzah.

Maror: Blessing for Bitter Herbs

READER: In preparation for eating *maror*, it is customary to dip the bitter
herbs into the sweet *charoset*—but not enough to take away from the taste
of bitterness. By doing so, we fulfill the second dipping referred to in the
Four Questions. Since *maror* is a symbol of bitter enslavement and reclining is a symbol of freedom, we do not recline when we eat *maror*.

Dip a small piece of maror *into the* charoset.

THE BLESSING

The blessing may be read or chanted in unison or by the Reader. The Reader also may read the blessing in Hebrew, one phrase at a time, with everyone joining in unison after each phrase and in the English, and then the blessing may be chanted.

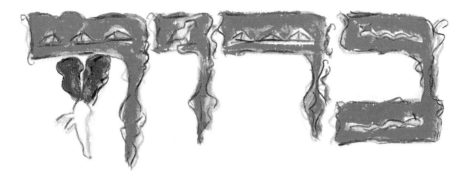

בָּרוּךְ אַתָּה, יְיָ אֱלֹהֵינוּ, מֶלֶךְ הָעוֹלָם,
אֲשֶׁר קִדְּשָׁנוּ, בְּמִצְוֹתָיו וְצִוָּנוּ, עַל אֲכִילַת מָרוֹר.

*Baruch atah, Adonai Eloheinu, Melech haolam,
asher kid'shanu, b'mitzvotav v'tzivanu, al achilat maror.*

Blessed are You, Eternal our God, Sovereign of the universe,
who has sanctified us with Your commandments and
has commanded us concerning the eating of bitter herbs.

Eat the maror that was dipped in the charoset.

Hillel's Sandwich

READER: To carry out the injunction "They shall eat it with unleavened bread and bitter herbs" (Numbers 9:11), our great sage Hillel (first century BCE) combined matzah and *maror* on Passover and ate them together. Tonight, we eat a sandwich of matzah, *maror,* and *charoset* to remember that in times of freedom, we must not forget the bitterness of slavery; and in times of oppression, we must keep alive the hope of freedom.

The bottom matzah on the seder plate is broken and distributed. Each person takes some maror *and* charoset, *places them on the matzah, and eats the sandwich.*

THE MEAL IS SERVED

קַדֵּשׁ
Kadeish
First Cup of Wine

וּרְחַץ
Urchatz
Washing Hands

כַּרְפַּס
Karpas
Green Vegetable

יַחַץ
Yachatz
Middle Matzah

מַגִּיד
Magid
Telling the Story

רָחְצָה
Rochtzah
Washing Hands
before the Meal

מוֹצִיא/מַצָּה
Motzi/Matzah
Matzah

מָרוֹר
Maror
Bitter Herbs

כּוֹרֵךְ
Koreich
Hillel Sandwich

שֻׁלְחָן עוֹרֵךְ
Shulchan Oreich
The Meal Is Served

צָפוּן
Tzafun
Afikoman

בָּרֵךְ
Bareich
Blessing After
the Meal

הַלֵּל
Hallel
Songs of Praise

נִרְצָה
Nirtzah
Conclusion

CONCLUDING
THE SEDER

Afikoman

Afikoman *is a Hebrew word based on a Greek word meaning "that which comes after the meal." After the meal, children search for the* afikoman. *(If no children are present, everyone may join the search.) When it is found and returned (sometimes for a reward), the* afikoman *is distributed and eaten by all present. The seder then continues. The* afikoman *is the last food to be eaten so that the taste and experience of the seder will stay with us until we come together and celebrate again next year.*

Birkat HaMazon: Blessing after the Meal

♫ *See appendix, page 89, for* Birkat HaMazon, *or use the following alternative blessing.*

AN ALTERNATIVE BLESSING

TOGETHER:

בָּרוּךְ אַתָּה, יְיָ, הַזָּן אֶת־הַכֹּל.

Baruch atah, Adonai, hazan et hakol.

We praise You, O God, Source of food for all who live.

Blessed are You, Eternal our God,
Sovereign of the universe, whose food we have eaten
and through whose goodness we live.

Blessed are You, Eternal our God, Sovereign of the universe,
who provides food for all and sustains the entire world
with goodness, kindness, and mercy.

O God, who sustains and protects us, be mindful of us today,
as You have been to our ancestors, so that we may find life
and peace as we celebrate the efforts of all people who seek
justice and freedom.

May the One who makes peace in the heavens let peace descend on all of us and all of Israel and throughout the world, and let us say: Amen.

A Moment of Torah

צָפוּן
Tzafun
Afikoman

בָּרֵךְ
Bareich
Blessing After
the Meal

הַלֵּל
Hallel
Songs of Praise

נִרְצָה
Nirtzah
Conclusion

READER: The Torah states that we should remember the day we left Egypt "all the days of your life" (Deuteronomy 16:3). Our Rabbis tell us that by adding the word "all" to the phrase "the *days* of your life" the Torah includes nights as well as days. Also, our Rabbis say that "the days of your life" refers to the world in which we live and the addition of the word "all" includes the messianic age (*Mishnah B'rachot* 1:5).

According to tradition, the prophet Elijah will announce the coming of the messianic age, a time when all peoples shall live in dignity, freedom, and peace. Even as we shall rejoice in the coming of the messianic age, so shall we remember even then our obligation to conduct a Passover seder each year and remember the day we left Egypt.

Blessing for the Third Cup of Wine

READER: Now we remember God's promise to our ancestors and to every generation:

"I will redeem you with an outstretched arm
and great acts of judgment." (Exodus 6:6)

וְגָאַלְתִּי אֶתְכֶם בִּזְרוֹעַ נְטוּיָה וּבִשְׁפָטִים גְּדֹלִים.

V'gaalti etchem bizroa n'tuyah uvishfatim g'dolim.

READER: As we drink the third cup of wine, we celebrate the holy bonds between family and friends and our sacred connection to all men, women, and children of every religion, race, and creed. May the goodwill in each of us draw us closer to one another, strengthening the ties between us so we may help each other through hard times as well as joyously celebrate good times together.

THE BLESSING

The blessing may be read or chanted in unison or by the Reader. The Reader may also read the blessing in Hebrew, one phrase at a time, with everyone joining in unison after each phrase and in the English, and then the blessing may be chanted.

READER: Together let us raise the third cup of wine and say:

Concluding
the Seder

62

Tzafun
Afikoman

בָּרֵךְ
Bareich
Blessing After
the Meal

הַלֵּל
Hallel
Songs of Praise

נִרְצָה
Nirtzah
Conclusion

🎵 בָּרוּךְ אַתָּה, יְיָ אֱלֹהֵינוּ, מֶלֶךְ הָעוֹלָם, בּוֹרֵא פְּרִי הַגָּפֶן.

Baruch atah, Adonai Eloheinu, Melech haolam,
borei p'ri hagafen.

Blessed are You, Eternal our God, Sovereign of the universe,
who has created the fruit of the vine.

Drink the third cup of wine, and refill the wine cups.

Opening the Door for Elijah

The person(s) who asked the Four Questions may be asked to read the part of the Child and open the door for Elijah.

Reader: As we approach the conclusion of our festive celebration, we fill Elijah's Cup with wine and prepare in hopeful anticipation to greet Elijah.

Fill Elijah's Cup with wine.

Child: Who is Elijah?

Reader: He was a prophet in Israel.

Child: Why does Elijah come?

Reader: He comes in answer to Israel's prayer. Again and again throughout history we have lived in exile and in tyranny when might has conquered right. In these darkest nights, our ancestors were comforted by the hope of the coming of the Messiah. They believed that the Messiah would bring a better world, a world in which Israel and all peoples would live in dignity and peace.

Child: When will this better world come?

the Seder

63

Reader: That is a mystery. Before the messianic day comes, however, the spirit of Elijah must live in the hearts of humankind. Our rabbis and sages teach that on Passover Elijah will come to announce the messianic age of peace and freedom. We open the door so that the prophet may enter.

The door is opened.

READER: We welcome Elijah with the ancient greeting.

Together or repeat after the Reader:

בָּרוּךְ הַבָּא בְּשֵׁם יְיָ.

Baruch haba b'sheim Adonai.

Blessed are you who comes in the name of the Eternal.

CHILD: Has Elijah come? We do not see him.

READER: Elijah cannot be seen. He comes as the goodness that is in the hearts of all people. He represents justice and peace. Just as it is our responsibility to open the door for Elijah at the seder, so too, does it remain our obligation to keep our hearts open to each other and the doors of freedom open for all. May God grant that next year all people may live together in freedom and peace.

BLESSING FOR ELIJAH

Together or repeat after the Reader:

בָּרוּךְ אַתָּה בְּבוֹאֶךָ, וּבָרוּךְ אַתָּה בְּצֵאתֶךָ.

Baruch atah b'vo-echa, u-varuch atah betzeitecha.

Blessed are you in your coming; blessed are you in your going.

Sung in Hebrew to traditional melody.

♫ אֵלִיָּהוּ הַנָּבִיא   ***ELIYAHU HANAVI***

אֵלִיָּהוּ הַנָּבִיא	*Eliyahu haNavi*
אֵלִיָּהוּ הַתִּשְׁבִּי,	*Eliyahu haTishbi,*
אֵלִיָּהוּ אֵלִיָּהוּ	*Eliyahu Eliyahu*
אֵלִיָּהוּ הַגִּלְעָדִי.	*Eliyahu haGiladi.*
בִּמְהֵרָה בְיָמֵינוּ	*Bimheirah v'yameinu*
יָבוֹא אֵלֵינוּ	*Yavo eileinu*
עִם מָשִׁיחַ בֶּן דָּוִד	*Im mashiach ben David*
עִם מָשִׁיחַ בֶּן דָּוִד.	*Im mashiach ben David.*
אֵלִיָּהוּ הַנָּבִיא	*Eliyahu haNavi*
אֵלִיָּהוּ הַתִּשְׁבִּי,	*Eliyahu haTishbi,*
אֵלִיָּהוּ אֵלִיָּהוּ	*Eliyahu Eliyahu*
אֵלִיָּהוּ הַגִּלְעָדִי.	*Eliyahu haGiladi.*

צָפוּן
Tzafun
Afikoman

בָּרֵךְ
Bareich
Blessing After
the Meal

הַלֵּל
Hallel
Songs of Praise

נִרְצָה
Nirtzah
Conclusion

May Elijah the Prophet,
Elijah the Tishbite,
Elijah of Gilead,
quickly in our day come to us
heralding redemption.

צָפוּן
Tzafun
Afikoman

בָּרֵךְ
Bareich
Blessing After
the Meal

הַלֵּל
Hallel
Songs of Praise

נִרְצָה
Nirtzah
Conclusion

We Give Thanks

Songs of Praise—Hallel (Psalms 115–118, page 92)—may be inserted here.

Read responsively:

As a community, we give thanks for the teachings of the story of Passover, which we shall remember all the days of our lives.

And for the symbols of Passover that inspire us to work for freedom for all.

As a community, we give thanks to God for our deliverance from bondage in Egypt and from those who have sought to destroy us in every age.

And for the reminder that in this world God's work to create the messianic age must truly be our own.

As a community, we give thanks for the love of family and for the gift of our extended family of friends and neighbors.

And for the experience of this Passover seder that brings us closer to God, to our families, and to one another.

We Share Our Blessings

READER: Tonight, we have opened our hearts to each other. We have sung songs, answered the Four Questions, offered blessings, and inspired one another in our study of God's teachings through the telling of the story of the Exodus.

We are blessed with life's sweetness and the knowledge of God's ways. We now give thanks for the many blessings we have received, with the prayer that everyone may soon share in them.

TOGETHER: With words of praise, we celebrate God's presence among us, now and in the days ahead, as we give thanks for the freedom we enjoy and our ability to come together and celebrate the Festival of Passover each year.

Blessing for the Fourth Cup of Wine

READER: Now we remember God's promise to our ancestors and to every generation:

"I will take you to be My people, and I will be your God."
(Exodus 6:7)

וְלָקַחְתִּי אֶתְכֶם לִי לְעָם וְהָיִיתִי לָכֶם לֵאלֹהִים.

V'lakachti etchem li l'am v'hayiti lachem leilohim.

READER: We dedicate the fourth cup of wine to *shalom*—to peace. May the One who broke Pharaoh's yoke forever shatter all fetters of oppression and hasten the day when swords shall, at last, be turned into plowshares and spears into pruning hooks. (Isaiah 2:4)

TOGETHER: May the State of Israel, all peoples in the Middle East, and peoples of every religion, race, and creed throughout the world soon experience the blessings of peace.

READER: May God be gracious to us and dispel the darkness of ignorance and prejudice from all peoples.

TOGETHER: May our country be a beacon of liberty and justice for all peoples. May we all be blessed with peace and freedom and be kept safe from danger everywhere.

THE BLESSING

The blessing may be read or chanted in unison or by the Reader. The Reader may also read the blessing in Hebrew, one phrase at a time, with everyone joining in unison after each phrase and in the English, and then the blessing may be chanted.

READER: Together let us raise the fourth cup of wine and say:

צָפוּן
Tzafun
Afikoman

בָּרֵךְ
Bareich
Blessing After
the Meal

הַלֵּל
Hallel
Songs of Praise

נִרְצָה
Nirtzah
Conclusion

בָּרוּךְ אַתָּה, יְיָ אֱלֹהֵינוּ, מֶלֶךְ הָעוֹלָם, בּוֹרֵא פְּרִי הַגָּפֶן.

Baruch atah, Adonai Eloheinu, Melech haolam,
borei p'ri hagafen.

Blessed are You, Eternal our God, Sovereign of the Universe,
who has created the fruit of the vine.

Drink the fourth cup of wine.

READER: Tonight we have given thanks to God by saying a blessing over four cups of wine as we celebrated the sanctity of every life, the survival of the Jewish people, the holiness of our bond to every family member, and the meaning of *shalom*—peace.

TOGETHER: May this seder provide us with new spirit and energy in the year ahead as we strive to meet the challenges to life's sweetness. May all peoples soon know freedom and peace!

Next Year in Jerusalem

READER: Jerusalem has symbolically been at the spiritual center of the lives of Jews, Christians, and Muslims for millennia. Each year our Passover seder renews our hope for the future. Tonight, we once again affirm our commitment to partner with God and join with one another to help repair the world. At the beginning of the messianic age, we look forward to rejoicing in Jerusalem with men, women, and children of all races, religions, and creeds to embrace as one family the blessings of peace and freedom. It is our prayer that it may be next year.

TOGETHER:

NEXT YEAR IN JERUSALEM!

לְשָׁנָה הַבָּאָה בִּירוּשָׁלָיִם!

Lashanah habaah birushalayim!

A Game and Songs to Close Our Seder

Echad Mi Yodei-a? / Who Knows One?
A Game for the End of the Seder (A creative interpretation of the
Hebrew found on page 102)

The Reader asks the questions, calling on persons to recite the answers in only one breath. (For the song ?אֶחָד מִי יוֹדֵעַ / Echad Mi Yodei-a? ("Who Knows One?") turn to page 102.)

Here are two versions, take your pick!

The Historic Version, from 1923

Who knows One? I know One: One God of the World.

Who knows Two? I know Two: Two Tablets of the Covenant; One God of the World.

Who knows Three? I know three: Three Patriarchs; Two Tablets of the Covenant; One God of the World.

Who knows Four? I know four: Four Mothers of Israel; Three Patriarchs; Two Tablets of the Covenant; One God of the World.

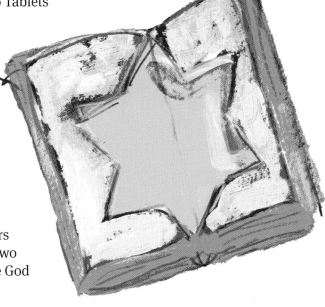

Who knows Five? I know Five: Five Books of Moses; Four Mothers of Israel; Three Patriarchs; Two Tablets of the Covenant; One God of the World.

Who knows Six? I know Six: Six Days of Creation; Five Books of Moses; Four Mothers of Israel; Three Patriarchs; Two Tablets of the Covenant; One God of the World.

Who knows Seven? I know Seven: Seven Days of the Week; Six Days of Creation; Five Books of Moses; Four Mothers of Israel; Three Patriarchs; Two Tablets of the Covenant; One God of the World.

Who knows Eight? I know Eight: Eight Lights of Chanukah; Seven Days of the Week; Six Days of Creation; Five Books of Moses; Four Mothers of Israel; Three Patriarchs; Two Tablets of the Covenant; One God of the World.

צָפוּן
Tzafun
Afikoman

בָּרֵךְ
Bareich
Blessing After
the Meal

הַלֵּל
Hallel
Songs of Praise

נִרְצָה
Nirtzah
Conclusion

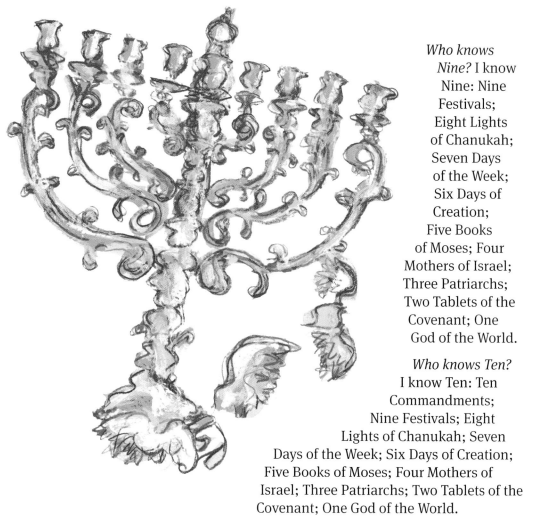

Who knows Nine? I know Nine: Nine Festivals; Eight Lights of Chanukah; Seven Days of the Week; Six Days of Creation; Five Books of Moses; Four Mothers of Israel; Three Patriarchs; Two Tablets of the Covenant; One God of the World.

Who knows Ten? I know Ten: Ten Commandments; Nine Festivals; Eight Lights of Chanukah; Seven Days of the Week; Six Days of Creation; Five Books of Moses; Four Mothers of Israel; Three Patriarchs; Two Tablets of the Covenant; One God of the World.

Who knows Eleven? I know Eleven: Eleven stars in Joseph's Dream; Ten Commandments; Nine Festivals; Eight Lights of Chanukah; Seven Days of the Week; Six Days of Creation; Five Books of Moses; Four Mothers of Israel; Three Patriarchs; Two Tablets of the Covenant; One God of the World.

Who knows Twelve? I know twelve: Twelve Tribes; Eleven Stars; Ten Commandments; Nine Festivals; Eight Lights of Chanukah; Seven Days of the Week; Six Days of Creation; Five Books of Moses; Four Mothers of Israel; Three Patriarchs; Two Tablets of the Covenant; One God of the World.

Who knows Thirteen? I know Thirteen: Thirteen Attributes of God; Twelve Tribes; Eleven Stars; Ten Commandments; Nine Festivals; Eight Lights of Chanukah; Seven Days of the Week; Six Days of Creation; Five Books of Moses; Four Mothers of Israel; Three Patriarchs; Two Tablets of the Covenant; One God of the World.

Who knows One? I know One. One is our God, in heaven and on earth.

Who knows Two? I know Two: Two are the tablets of the Covenant. One is our God, in heaven and on earth.

צָפוּן
Tzafun
Afikoman

בָּרֵךְ
Bareich
Blessing After
the Meal

הַלֵּל
Hallel
Songs of Praise

נִרְצָה
Nirtzah
Conclusion

Who knows Three? I know Three: Three are the patriarchs. Two are the tablets of the Covenant. One is our God, in heaven and on earth.

Who knows Four? I know Four: Four are the matriarchs. Three are the patriarchs. Two are the tablets of the Covenant. One is our God, in heaven and on earth.

Who knows Five? I know Five: Five are the books of the Torah. Four are the matriarchs. Three are the patriarchs. Two are the tablets of the Covenant. One is our God, in heaven and on earth.

Who knows Six? I know Six: Six are the orders of the Mishnah. Five are the books of the Torah. Four are the matriarchs. Three are the patriarchs. Two are the tablets of the Covenant. One is our God, in heaven and on earth.

Who knows Seven? I know Seven: Seven are the days of the week. Six are the orders of the Mishnah. Five are the books of the Torah. Four are the matriarchs. Three are the patriarchs. Two are the tablets of the Covenant. One is our God, in heaven and on earth.

Who knows Eight? I know Eight: Eight are the days until circumcision. Seven are the days of the week. Six are the orders of the Mishnah. Five are the books of the Torah. Four are the matriarchs. Three are the patriarchs. Two are the tablets of the Covenant. One is our God, in heaven and on earth.

Who knows Nine? I know Nine: Nine are the months of pregnancy. Eight are the days until circumcision. Seven are the days of the week. Six are the orders of the Mishnah. Five are the books of the Torah. Four are the matriarchs. Three are the patriarchs. Two are the tablets of the Covenant. One is our God, in heaven and on earth.

Who knows Ten? I know Ten: Ten are the Commandments. Nine are the months of pregnancy. Eight are the days until circumcision. Seven are the days of the week. Six are the orders of the Mishnah. Five are the books of the Torah. Four are the matriarchs. Three are the patriarchs. Two are the tablets of the Covenant. One is our God, in heaven and on earth.

Who knows Eleven? I know Eleven: Eleven are the stars in Joseph's dream. Ten are the Commandments. Nine are the months of pregnancy. Eight are the days until circumcision. Seven are the days of the week.

Six are the orders of the Mishnah. Five are the books of the Torah. Four are the matriarchs. Three are the patriarchs. Two are the tablets of the Covenant. One is our God, in heaven and on earth.

Who knows Twelve? I know twelve: Twelve are the tribes of Israel. Eleven are the stars in Joseph's dream. Ten are the Commandments. Nine are the months of pregnancy. Eight are the days until circumcision. Seven are the days of the week. Six are the orders of the Mishnah. Five are the books of the Torah. Four are the matriarchs. Three are the patriarchs. Two are the tablets of the Covenant. One is our God, in heaven and on earth.

Who knows Thirteen? I know Thirteen. Thirteen are the attributes of God. Twelve are the tribes of Israel. Eleven are the stars in Joseph's dream. Ten are the Commandments. Nine are the months of pregnancy. Eight are the days until circumcision. Seven are the days of the week. Six are the orders of the Mishnah. Five are the books of the Torah. Four are the matriarchs. Three are the patriarchs. Two are the tablets of the Covenant. One is our God, in heaven and on earth.

צָפוּן
Tzafun
Afikoman

בָּרֵךְ
Bareich
Blessing After the Meal

הַלֵּל
Hallel
Songs of Praise

נִרְצָה
Nirtzah
Conclusion

CHAD GADYA / AN ONLY KID
A Poem/Song for the End of the Seder

Chad gadya, chad gadya.
My father bought, for two zuzim.

Chad gadya, chad gadya

Then came the cat, and ate the kid
My father bought for two zuzim.

Chad gadya, chad gadya

Then came the dog, and bit the cat, that ate the kid
My father bought for two zuzim.

Chad gadya, chad gadya

Then came the stick, and beat the dog, that bit the cat,
that ate the kid, my father bought for two zuzim.

Chad gadya, chad gadya

Then came the fire, and burned the stick,
that beat the dog, that bit the cat, that ate the kid,
my father bought for two zuzim.

Chad gadya, chad gadya

Concluding
the Seder

Then came the water, and quenched the fire, that burned the stick, that beat the dog, that bit the cat, that ate the kid, my father bought for two zuzim.

Chad gadya, chad gadya

Then came the ox, and drank the water, that quenched the fire, that burned the stick, that beat the dog, that bit the cat, that ate the kid, my father bought for two zuzim.

Chad gadya, chad gadya

Then came the butcher, and killed the ox, that drank the water, that quenched the fire, that burned the stick, that beat the dog, that bit the cat, that ate the kid, my father bought for two zuzim.

Chad gadya, chad gadya

Then came the angel of death, and slew the butcher, that killed the ox, that drank the water, that quenched the fire, that burned the stick, that beat the dog, that bit the cat, that ate the kid, my father bought for two zuzim.

Chad gadya, chad gadya

Then came the Holy One—blessed be God—and destroyed the angel of death, that slew the butcher, that killed the ox, that drank the water, that quenched the fire, that burned the stick, that beat the dog, that bit the cat, that ate the kid, my father bought for two zuzim.

Chad gadya, chad gadya

חַד גַּדְיָא   *CHAD GADYA*   🎵

חַד גַּדְיָא, חַד גַּדְיָא,
דְּזַבִּן אַבָּא בִּתְרֵי זוּזֵי.

*Chad gadya, chad gadya,
dizvan aba bitrei zuzei.*

חַד גַּדְיָא, חַד גַּדְיָא.

Chad gadya, chad gadya.

וַאֲתָא שׁוּנְרָא, וְאָכַל לְגַדְיָא,
דְּזַבִּן אַבָּא בִּתְרֵי זוּזֵי.

*Vaata shunra, v'achal l'gadya,
dizvan aba bitrei zuzei.*

חַד גַּדְיָא, חַד גַּדְיָא.

Chad gadya, chad gadya.

וַאֲתָא כַלְבָּא,
וְנָשַׁךְ לְשׁוּנְרָא,
דְּאָכַל לְגַדְיָא,
דְּזַבִּן אַבָּא בִּתְרֵי זוּזֵי.

*Vaata chalba,
v'nashach l'shunrah,
d'achal l'gadya,
dizvan aba bitrei zuzei.*

Chad Gadya *is called a "cumulative song," a song that gets longer and longer with each verse. Its origins, while obscure, can be traced back to the thirteenth century. Some claim that it is an allegory for the fate of the nations that have ruled over the Jewish people throughout history, but its original intentions are not known. Songs like* Chad Gadya, *sung at the end of the seder, are a reflection of the historic Jewish desire to poetically express our praise of God. They are also a good way to keep the children engaged and interested.*

צָפוּן
Tzafun
Afikoman

בָּרֵךְ
Bareich
Blessing After
the Meal

הַלֵּל
Hallel
Songs of Praise

נִרְצָה
Nirtzah
Conclusion

חַד גַּדְיָא, חַד גַּדְיָא.   *Chad gadya, chad gadya.*

וַאֲתָא חוּטְרָא, וְהִכָּה לְכַלְבָּא,   *Vaata chutra, v'hikah l'chalba,*
דְּנָשַׁךְ לְשׁוּנְרָא,   *d'nashach l'shunra,*
דְּאָכַל לְגַדְיָא,   *d'achal l'gadya,*
דִּזְבַן אַבָּא בִּתְרֵי זוּזֵי.   *dizvan aba bitrei zuzei.*

חַד גַּדְיָא, חַד גַּדְיָא.   *Chad gadya, chad gadya.*

וַאֲתָא נוּרָא, וְשָׂרַף לְחוּטְרָא,   *Vaata nurah, v'saraf l'chutra,*
דְּהִכָּה לְכַלְבָּא,   *d'hikah l'chalba,*
דְּנָשַׁךְ לְשׁוּנְרָא,   *d'nashach l'shunra,*
דְּאָכַל לְגַדְיָא,   *d'achal l'gadya,*
דִּזְבַן אַבָּא בִּתְרֵי זוּזֵי.   *dizvan aba bitrei zuzei.*

חַד גַּדְיָא, חַד גַּדְיָא.   *Chad gadya, chad gadya.*

וַאֲתָא מַיָּא, וְכָבָה לְנוּרָא,   *Vaata maya, v'chavah l'nura,*
דְּשָׂרַף לְחוּטְרָא,   *d'saraf l'chutra,*
דְּהִכָּה לְכַלְבָּא,   *d'hikah l'chalba,*
דְּנָשַׁךְ לְשׁוּנְרָא,   *d'nashach l'shunra,*
דְּאָכַל לְגַדְיָא,   *d'achal l'gadya,*
דִּזְבַן אַבָּא בִּתְרֵי זוּזֵי.   *dizvan aba bitrei zuzei.*

חַד גַּדְיָא, חַד גַּדְיָא.   *Chad gadya, chad gadya.*

וַאֲתָא תוֹרָא, וְשָׁתָה לְמַיָּא,   *Vaata tora, v'shatah l'maya,*
דְּכָבָה לְנוּרָא,   *d'chavah l'nura,*
דְּשָׂרַף לְחוּטְרָא, דְּהִכָּה לְכַלְבָּא,   *d'saraf l'chutra, d'hikah l'chalba,*
דְּנָשַׁךְ לְשׁוּנְרָא,   *d'nashach l'shunra,*
דְּאָכַל לְגַדְיָא,   *d'achal l'gadya,*
דִּזְבַן אַבָּא בִּתְרֵי זוּזֵי.   *dizvan aba bitrei zuzei.*

חַד גַּדְיָא, חַד גַּדְיָא.   *Chad gadya, chad gadya.*

וַאֲתָא הַשּׁוֹחֵט, וְשָׁחַט לְתוֹרָא,   *Vaata hashocheit, v'shachat l'tora,*
דְּשָׁתָה לְמַיָּא, דְּכָבָה לְנוּרָא,   *d'shatah l'maya, d'chavah l'nura,*
דְּשָׂרַף לְחוּטְרָא, דְּהִכָּה לְכַלְבָּא,   *d'saraf l'chutra, d'hikah l'chalba,*
דְּנָשַׁךְ לְשׁוּנְרָא,   *d'nashach l'shunra,*
דְּאָכַל לְגַדְיָא,   *d'achal l'gadya,*
דִּזְבַן אַבָּא בִּתְרֵי זוּזֵי.   *dizvan aba bitrei zuzei.*

חַד גַּדְיָא, חַד גַּדְיָא.   *Chad gadya, chad gadya.*

וַאֲתָא מַלְאַךְ הַמָּוֶת,   *Vaata malach hamavet,*

וְשָׁחַט לַשּׁוֹחֵט,   *v'shachat lashocheit,*

דְּשָׁחַט לְתוֹרָא, דְּשָׁתָה לְמַיָּא,   *d'shachat l'tora, d'shatah l'maya,*

דְּכָבָה לְנוּרָא, דְּשָׂרַף לְחוּטְרָא,   *d'chavah l'nura, d'saraf l'chutra,*

דְּהִכָּה לְכַלְבָּא,   *d'hikah l'chalba,*

דְּנָשַׁךְ לְשׁוּנְרָא,   *d'nashach l'shunra,*

דְּאָכַל לְגַדְיָא,   *d'achal l'gadya,*

דְּזַבַּן אַבָּא בִּתְרֵי זוּזֵי.   *dizvan aba bitrei zuzei.*

חַד גַּדְיָא, חַד גַּדְיָא.   *Chad gadya, chad gadya.*

וַאֲתָא הַקָּדוֹשׁ בָּרוּךְ הוּא,   *Vaata hakadosh baruch hu,*

וְשָׁחַט לְמַלְאַךְ הַמָּוֶת,   *v'shachat l'malach hamavet,*

דְּשָׁחַט לַשּׁוֹחֵט,   *d'shachat lashocheit,*

דְּשָׁחַט לְתוֹרָא,   *d'shachat l'tora,*

דְּשָׁתָה לְמַיָּא, דְּכָבָה לְנוּרָא,   *d'shatah l'maya, d'chavah l'nura,*

דְּשָׂרַף לְחוּטְרָא, דְּהִכָּה לְכַלְבָּא,   *d'saraf l'chutra, d'hikah l'chalba,*

דְּנָשַׁךְ לְשׁוּנְרָא,   *d'nashach l'shunra,*

דְּאָכַל לְגַדְיָא,   *d'achal l'gadya,*

דְּזַבַּן אַבָּא בִּתְרֵי זוּזֵי.   *dizvan aba bitrei zuzei.*

חַד גַּדְיָא, חַד גַּדְיָא.   *Chad gadya, chad gadya.*

צָפוּן
Tzafun
Afikoman

בָּרֵךְ
Bareich
Blessing After
the Meal

הַלֵּל
Hallel
Songs of Praise

נִרְצָה
Nirtzah
Conclusion

GOD OF MIGHT
A Song for the End of the Seder

God of Might, God of Right,
Thee we give all glory;
Thine all praise in these days,
As in ages hoary;
When we hear, year by year,
Freedom's wondrous story.

Now as erst, when Thou first
Made the proclamation,
Warning loud every proud,
Every tyrant nation,
We, Thy fame still proclaim,
Bend in adoration.

Concluding
the Seder

78

Be with all, who in thrall
To their tasks are driven;
By Thy power speed the hour
When their chains are riven;
Earth around will resound
Joyful hymns to heaven.

אַדִּיר הוּא   *ADIR HU*   ♫

אַדִּיר הוּא, אַדִּיר הוּא,	Adir hu, adir hu,
יִבְנֶה בֵיתוֹ בְּקָרוֹב,	Yivneh veito b'karov,
בִּמְהֵרָה בִּמְהֵרָה,	Bimheirah, bimheirah,
בְּיָמֵינוּ בְּקָרוֹב.	B'yameinu b'karov.
אֵל בְּנֵה, אֵל בְּנֵה,	El b'neih, El b'neih,
בְּנֵה בֵיתְךָ בְּקָרוֹב.	B'neih veitcha b'karov.

בָּחוּר הוּא, גָּדוֹל הוּא,	Bachur hu, gadol hu,
דָּגוּל הוּא,	dagul hu,
יִבְנֶה בֵיתוֹ בְּקָרוֹב . . .	Yivneh veito b'karov . . .

הָדוּר הוּא, וָתִיק הוּא,	Hadur hu, vatik hu,
זַכַּאי הוּא, חָסִיד הוּא,	zakai hu, chasid hu,
יִבְנֶה בֵיתוֹ בְּקָרוֹב . . .	Yivneh veito b'karov . . .

טָהוֹר הוּא, יָחִיד הוּא,	Tahor hu, yachid hu,
כַּבִּיר הוּא, לָמוּד הוּא,	kabir hu, lamud hu,
מֶלֶךְ הוּא, נוֹרָא הוּא,	melech hu, norah hu,
סַגִּיב הוּא, עִזּוּז הוּא,	sagiv hu, izuz hu,
פּוֹדֶה הוּא, צַדִּיק הוּא,	podeh hu, tzaddik hu
יִבְנֶה בֵיתוֹ בְּקָרוֹב . . .	Yivneh veito b'karov . . .

קָדוֹשׁ הוּא, רַחוּם הוּא,	Kadosh hu, rachum hu,
שַׁדַּי הוּא, תַּקִּיף הוּא,	shadai hu, takif hu
יִבְנֶה בֵיתוֹ בְּקָרוֹב . . .	Yivneh veito b'karov . . .

Mighty is God, mighty is God

May God's house be built soon
Speedily, speedily and in our days, soon
God rebuild! God rebuild!
Rebuild Your house soon!

צָפוּן
Tzafun
Afikoman

בָּרֵךְ
Bareich
Blessing After
the Meal

הַלֵּל
Hallel
Songs of Praise

נִרְצָה
Nirtzah
Conclusion

*The praises
of God in this
song form an
alphabetized
acrostic. The
first Hebrew
letter of the
words indicatd
in bold are in
the order of
the Hebrew
alphabet.*

God is distinguished, God is great,
God is exalted

May God's house be built soon
Speedily, speedily and in our days, soon
God rebuild! God rebuild!
Rebuild Your house soon!

God is glorious, God is faithful,
God is faultless, God is righteous

May God's house be built soon
Speedily, speedily and in our days, soon
God rebuild! God rebuild!
Rebuild Your house soon!

God is pure, God is unique, God is powerful,
God is wise, God is Sovereign, God is revered,
God is sublime, God is all-powerful,
God is Redeemer, God is all-righteous

May God's house be built soon
Speedily, speedily and in our days, soon
God rebuild! God rebuild!
Rebuild Your house soon!

God is holy, God is compassionate,
God is almighty, God is omnipotent

May God's house be built soon
Speedily, speedily and in our days, soon
God rebuild! God rebuild!
Rebuild Your house soon!

צָפוּן
Tzafun
Afikoman

בָּרֵךְ
Bareich
Blessing After
the Meal

הַלֵּל
Hallel
Songs of Praise

נִרְצָה
Nirtzah
Conclusion

Appendix

SONGS TO BEGIN THE SEDER

Optional song by Ron Wolfson, sung to the tune of "Take Me Out to the Ball Game."

TAKE US OUT OF EGYPT

Take us out of Egypt
Free us from slavery
Bake us some matzah in a haste
Don't worry about flavor—
Give no thought to taste

Oh its rush, rush, rush to the Red Sea
If we don't cross it's a shame
For it's ten plagues,
Down and you're out
At the Pesach history game.

Optional song, sung to the tune of "Take Me Out to the Ball Game."

TAKE ME OUT TO THE SEDER

Take me out to the seder
With friends and family
Serve me matzah and four cups of wine,
Ask me four questions and we will be fine.

And its root, root, root for Elijah
That he will soon reappear.
And let's hope, hope, hope that we'll meet
Once again next year!

And let's hope, hope, hope that we'll meet
Once again next year!

SUPPLEMENTAL BLESSINGS

Festival *Kiddush:* **Blessing for the First Cup of Wine**

The person leading the blessing raises his/her cup.

READER: With song and praise, and with the symbols of Passover, let us renew the memories of our past. In love God has given us solemn days of joy and this Festival season of Passover, a remembrance of our departure from Egypt and a celebration of freedom and life.

On Shabbat, add the text in parentheses.

(וַיְהִי עֶרֶב, וַיְהִי בְקֶר,
יוֹם הַשִּׁשִּׁי. וַיְכֻלּוּ הַשָּׁמַיִם וְהָאָרֶץ וְכָל־צְבָאָם.
וַיְכַל אֱלֹהִים בַּיּוֹם הַשְּׁבִיעִי מְלַאכְתּוֹ אֲשֶׁר עָשָׂה,
וַיִּשְׁבֹּת בַּיּוֹם הַשְּׁבִיעִי מִכָּל־מְלַאכְתּוֹ אֲשֶׁר עָשָׂה.
וַיְבָרֶךְ אֱלֹהִים אֶת־יוֹם הַשְּׁבִיעִי וַיְקַדֵּשׁ אֹתוֹ,
כִּי בוֹ שָׁבַת מִכָּל־מְלַאכְתּוֹ, אֲשֶׁר בָּרָא אֱלֹהִים לַעֲשׂוֹת.)

(Vay'hi erev, vay'hi voker, yom hashishi.
Vaychulu hashamayim v'haaretz v'chol tz'vaam.
Vaychal Elohim bayom hash'vi-i m'lachto asher asah.
Vayishbot bayom hash'vi-i mikol m'lachto asher asah.
Vayvarech Elohim et yom hash'vi-i vay'kadeish oto,
ki vo shavat mikol m'lachto, asher bara Elohim laasot.)

(It was evening and it was morning, the sixth day.
The heavens and the earth and all they contained were
completed. And on the seventh day God rested from all the
work of creation. And God blessed the seventh day
and made it holy, because it was the day God rested from
all the work of creation.)

Let us together raise our first cup of wine and say:

♫ בָּרוּךְ אַתָּה, יְיָ אֱלֹהֵינוּ, מֶלֶךְ הָעוֹלָם, בּוֹרֵא פְּרִי הַגָּפֶן.

Baruch atah, Adonai Eloheinu, Melech haolam,
borei p'ri hagafen.

Blessed are You, Eternal our God, Sovereign of the universe,
Creator of the fruit of the vine.

בָּרוּךְ אַתָּה, יְיָ אֱלֹהֵינוּ, מֶלֶךְ הָעוֹלָם, אֲשֶׁר בָּחַר בָּנוּ
מִכָּל־עָם, וְרוֹמְמָנוּ מִכָּל־לָשׁוֹן, וְקִדְּשָׁנוּ בְּמִצְוֹתָיו.

וַתִּתֶּן־לָנוּ, יְיָ אֱלֹהֵינוּ, בְּאַהֲבָה (שַׁבָּתוֹת לִמְנוּחָה וּ) מוֹ
עֲדִים לְשִׂמְחָה, חַגִּים וּזְמַנִּים לְשָׂשׂוֹן,

אֶת־יוֹם (הַשַּׁבָּת הַזֶּה וְאֶת יוֹם) חַג הַמַּצּוֹת הַזֶּה, זְמַן
חֵרוּתֵנוּ (בְּאַהֲבָה) מִקְרָא־קֹדֶשׁ, זֵכֶר לִיצִיאַת מִצְרָיִם.

כִּי בָנוּ בָחַרְתָּ וְאוֹתָנוּ קִדַּשְׁתָּ מִכָּל־הָעַמִּים,

(וְשַׁבָּת וּ) מוֹעֲדֵי קָדְשֶׁךָ (בְּאַהֲבָה וּבְרָצוֹן) בְּשִׂמְחָה
וּבְשָׂשׂוֹן הִנְחַלְתָּנוּ. בָּרוּךְ אַתָּה, יְיָ, מְקַדֵּשׁ (הַשַּׁבָּת וְ)
יִשְׂרָאֵל וְהַזְּמַנִּים.

Baruch atah, Adonai Eloheinu, Melech haolam,
asher bachar banu mikol am, v'rom'manu mikol lashon,
v'kid'shanu b'mitzvotav.

Vatiten lanu, Adonai Eloheinu, b'ahavah (Shabbatot
limnuchah u) mo-adim l'simchah, chagim uzmanim l'sason, et
yom (HaShabbat hazeh v'et yom) Chag HaMatzot hazeh, z'man
cheiruteinu (b'ahavah) mikra kodesh, zeicher litziat Mitzrayim.

Ki vanu vacharta v'otanu kidashta mikol haamim (v'Shabbat)
umo-adei kodsh'cha (b'ahavah uvratzon) b'simchah uv'sason
hinchaltanu.

Baruch atah, Adonai, m'kadeish (haShabbat v') Yisrael
v'haz'manim.

Blessed are you, Eternal our God, Sovereign of the universe,
Creator of the fruit of the vine. Blessed are You, Adonai our
God, Sovereign of the universe, who has chosen us from
among the peoples, exalting us by hallowing us with mitzvot.
In Your love, Adonai our God, You have given us (Shabbatot of
rest), feasts of gladness, and seasons of joy: this (Shabbat day

and this) Festival of Pesach, season of our freedom, a sacred
occasion, a remembrance of the Exodus from Egypt. For You
have chosen us from all the peoples and consecrated us to
Your service, and given us (Shabbat, a sign of love and favor,
and) the Festivals, a time of gladness and joy. Blessed are You,
Adonai, who sancifies (Shabbat and) Israel and the festivals.

Drink the first cup of wine.

When the seder falls on a Saturday night, add the following blessings for Havdalah.

בָּרוּךְ אַתָּה, יְיָ אֱלֹהֵינוּ, מֶלֶךְ הָעוֹלָם, בּוֹרֵא מְאוֹרֵי הָאֵשׁ.

*Baruch atah, Adonai Eloheinu, Melech haolom,
borei m'orei ha-eish.*

Blessed are You, Eternal our God, Sovereign of the universe,
Creator of the fire's light.

בָּרוּךְ אַתָּה, יְיָ אֱלֹהֵינוּ, מֶלֶךְ הָעוֹלָם, הַמַּבְדִּיל בֵּין קֹדֶשׁ לְחֹל
בֵּין אוֹר לְחֹשֶׁךְ, בֵּין יִשְׂרָאֵל לָעַמִּים, בֵּין יוֹם הַשְּׁבִיעִי לְשֵׁשֶׁת
יְמֵי הַמַּעֲשֶׂה. בֵּין קְדֻשַּׁת שַׁבָּת לִקְדֻשַּׁת יוֹם טוֹב הִבְדַּלְתָּ.
וְאֶת־יוֹם הַשְּׁבִיעִי מִשֵּׁשֶׁת יְמֵי הַמַּעֲשֶׂה קִדַּשְׁתָּ. הִבְדַּלְתָּ
וְקִדַּשְׁתָּ אֶת־עַמְּךָ יִשְׂרָאֵל בִּקְדֻשָּׁתֶךָ. בָּרוּךְ אַתָּה, יְיָ, הַמַּבְדִּיל
בֵּין קֹדֶשׁ לְקֹדֶשׁ.

*Baruch atah, Adonai Eloheinu, Melech haolam, hamavdil bein
kodesh l'chol, bein or l'choshech, bein Yisrael laamin, bein yom
hash'vi-i l'sheishet y'mei hamaaseh. Bein k'dushat Shabbat
lik'dushat yom tov hivdalta. V'et yom hash'vi-i misheishet
y'mei hamaaseh kidashta. Hivdalta v'kidashta et am'cha
Yisrael bik'dushatecha. Baruch atah, Adonai, hamavdil bein
kodesh l'kodesh.*

Blessed are You, Eternal our God, Sovereign of the universe,
You distinguish between the holy and the ordinary, between
light and darkness, between Israel and the nations, between
the seventh day and the six days of Creation, between the
holiness of Shabbat and the holiness of the Festival Day.
You sanctify the seventh day from the six days of Creation.
You distinguish and make holy Your people Israel. Blessed
are You, Adonai our God, who distinguishes between
holiness and holiness.

Continue with Shehechyanu *on page 23.*

Blessing after the Meal: *Birkat HaMazon*

♫ בִּרְכַּת הַמָּזוֹן *BIRKAT HAMAZON*

שִׁיר הַמַּעֲלוֹת, בְּשׁוּב יְיָ	*Shir hamaalot, b'shuv Adonai*
אֶת־שִׁיבַת צִיּוֹן, הָיִינוּ כְּחֹלְמִים.	*et shivat Tziyon, hayinu k'cholmim.*
אָז יִמָּלֵא שְׂחוֹק פִּינוּ,	*Az yimalei s'chok pinu,*
וּלְשׁוֹנֵנוּ רִנָּה.	*ul'shoneinu rinah.*
אָז יֹאמְרוּ בַגּוֹיִם,	*Az yomru vagoyim,*
הִגְדִּיל יְיָ לַעֲשׂוֹת עִם אֵלֶּה.	*higdil Adonai laasot im eileh.*
הִגְדִּיל יְיָ לַעֲשׂוֹת עִמָּנוּ,	*Higdil Adonai laasot imanu,*
הָיִינוּ שְׂמֵחִים.	*hayinu s'meichim.*
שׁוּבָה יְיָ אֶת־שְׁבִיתֵנוּ	*Shuvah Adonai et sh'viteinu*
כַּאֲפִיקִים בַּנֶּגֶב.	*kaafikim banegev.*
הַזֹּרְעִים בְּדִמְעָה, בְּרִנָּה יִקְצֹרוּ.	*Hazorim b'dimah b'rinah yiktzoru.*
הָלוֹךְ יֵלֵךְ וּבָכֹה	*Haloch yeileich uvachoh*
נֹשֵׂא מֶשֶׁךְ־הַזָּרַע	*nosei meshech hazara,*
בֹּא יָבֹא בְרִנָּה נֹשֵׂא אֲלֻמֹּתָיו.	*bo yavo v'rinah, nosei alumotav.*

Leader:

חֲבֵרִים וַחֲבֵרוֹת, נְבָרֵךְ!	*Chaveirim vachaveirot, n'vareich!*

Together:

יְהִי שֵׁם יְיָ מְבֹרָךְ	*Y'hi sheim Adonai m'vorach*
מֵעַתָּה וְעַד עוֹלָם.	*mei-atah v'ad olam.*

Leader:

יְהִי שֵׁם יְיָ מְבֹרָךְ	*Y'hi sheim Adonai m'vorach*
מֵעַתָּה וְעַד עוֹלָם.	*mei-atah v'ad olam.*
בִּרְשׁוּת הַחֶבְרָה, נְבָרֵךְ	*Bir'shut hachevrah, n'vareich*
(אֱלֹהֵינוּ)	*(Eloheinu)*
שֶׁאָכַלְנוּ מִשֶּׁלוֹ.	*she-achalnu mishelo.*

Together:

בָּרוּךְ (אֱלֹהֵינוּ)	*Baruch (Eloheinu)*
שֶׁאָכַלְנוּ מִשֶּׁלוֹ	*she-achalnu mishelo*
וּבְטוּבוֹ חָיִינוּ.	*uvtuvo chayinu.*
בָּרוּךְ (אֱלֹהֵינוּ)	*Baruch (Eloheinu)*
שֶׁאָכַלְנוּ מִשֶּׁלוֹ	*she-achalnu mishelo*

וּבְטוּבוֹ חָיִינוּ.	uv'tuvo chayinu.
בָּרוּךְ הוּא וּבָרוּךְ שְׁמוֹ.	Baruch hu uvaruch sh'mo.

Together:

בָּרוּךְ אַתָּה, יְיָ אֱלֹהֵינוּ,	Baruch atah, Adonai Eloheinu,
מֶלֶךְ הָעוֹלָם, הַזָּן אֶת הָעוֹלָם	Melech haolam, hazan et haolam
כֻּלּוֹ בְּטוּבוֹ בְּחֵן	kulo b'tuvo, b'chein
בְּחֶסֶד וּבְרַחֲמִים.	b'chesed uv'rachamim.
הוּא נוֹתֵן לֶחֶם לְכָל־בָּשָׂר,	Hu notein lechem l'chol basar,
כִּי לְעוֹלָם חַסְדּוֹ.	ki l'olam chasdo.
וּבְטוּבוֹ הַגָּדוֹל	Uvtuvo hagadol
תָּמִיד לֹא חָסַר לָנוּ,	tamid lo chasar lanu,
וְאַל יֶחְסַר־לָנוּ מָזוֹן	v'al yechsar lanu mazon
לְעוֹלָם וָעֶד.	l'olam va-ed.
בַּעֲבוּר שְׁמוֹ הַגָּדוֹל,	Baavur sh'mo hagadol,
כִּי הוּא זָן וּמְפַרְנֵס לַכֹּל,	ki hu zan um'farneis lakol,
וּמֵטִיב לַכֹּל, וּמֵכִין מָזוֹן	umeitiv lakol, umeichin mazon
לְכָל־בְּרִיּוֹתָיו אֲשֶׁר בָּרָא.	l'chol b'riyotav asher bara.
בָּרוּךְ אַתָּה, יְיָ,	Baruch atah, Adonai,
הַזָּן אֶת־הַכֹּל.	hazan et hakol.
כַּכָּתוּב: וְאָכַלְתָּ וְשָׂבָעְתָּ,	Kakatuv: v'achalta v'savata,
וּבֵרַכְתָּ אֶת־יְיָ אֱלֹהֶיךָ	uveirachta et Adonai Elohecha
עַל הָאָרֶץ הַטּוֹבָה	al haaretz hatovah
אֲשֶׁר נָתַן לָךְ.	asher natan lach.
בָּרוּךְ אַתָּה, יְיָ,	Baruch atah, Adonai,
עַל הָאָרֶץ וְעַל הַמָּזוֹן.	al haaretz v'al hamazon.
וּבְנֵה יְרוּשָׁלַיִם עִיר הַקֹּדֶשׁ	Uv'neih Y'rushalayim ir hakodesh
בִּמְהֵרָה בְיָמֵינוּ.	bimheirah v'yameinu.
בָּרוּךְ אַתָּה, יְיָ,	Baruch atah, Adonai,
בּוֹנֵה בְרַחֲמָיו יְרוּשָׁלָיִם.	boneh v'rachamav Y'rushalayim.
אָמֵן.	Amein.
הָרַחֲמָן, הוּא יִמְלוֹךְ עָלֵינוּ	Harachaman, hu yimloch aleinu
לְעוֹלָם וָעֶד.	l'olam va-ed.
הָרַחֲמָן, הוּא יִתְבָּרַךְ	Harachaman, hu yitbarach
בַּשָּׁמַיִם וּבָאָרֶץ.	bashamayim u'vaaretz.

90

הָרַחֲמָן, הוּא יִשְׁלַח בְּרָכָה
מְרֻבָּה בַּבַּיִת הַזֶּה,
וְעַל שֻׁלְחָן זֶה שֶׁאָכַלְנוּ עָלָיו.

Harachaman, hu yishlach b'rachah
m'rubah babayit hazeh,
v'al shulchan zeh she-achalnu alav.

הָרַחֲמָן,
הוּא יִשְׁלַח לָנוּ
אֶת אֵלִיָּהוּ הַנָּבִיא,
זָכוּר לַטּוֹב,
וִיבַשֶּׂר־לָנוּ בְּשׂוֹרוֹת טוֹבוֹת,
יְשׁוּעוֹת וְנֶחָמוֹת.

Harachaman,
hu yishlach lanu
et Eiliyahu HaNavi,
zachur latov,
vivaser lanu b'sorot tovot,
y'shuot v'nechamot.

(On Shabbat):

(הָרַחֲמָן,
הוּא יַנְחִילֵנוּ יוֹם
שֶׁכֻּלּוֹ שַׁבָּת וּמְנוּחָה
לְחַיֵּי הָעוֹלָמִים.)

(Harachaman,
hu yanchileinu yom
shekulo Shabbat um'nuchah
l'chayei haolamim.)

הָרַחֲמָן,
הוּא יַנְחִילֵנוּ יוֹם
שֶׁכֻּלּוֹ טוֹב.

Harachaman,
hu yanchileinu yom
shekulo tov.

עֹשֶׂה שָׁלוֹם בִּמְרוֹמָיו,
הוּא יַעֲשֶׂה שָׁלוֹם,
עָלֵינוּ וְעַל כָּל יִשְׂרָאֵל,
וְעַל כָּל יוֹשְׁבֵי תֵבֵל,
וְאִמְרוּ אָמֵן.

Oseh shalom bim'romav,
hu yaaseh shalom,
aleinu v'al kol Yisrael,
v'al kol yosh'vei teiveil,
v'imru amen.

יְיָ עֹז לְעַמּוֹ יִתֵּן,
יְיָ יְבָרֵךְ אֶת
עַמּוֹ בַשָּׁלוֹם.

Adonai oz l'amo yitein,
Adonai y'vareich et
amo vashalom.

PSALMS

Hallel—Songs of Praise: Psalms 115–118

PSALM 115

Not to us, Adonai, not to us
but to Your name bring glory
for the sake of Your love and Your faithfulness.
Let the nations not say,
"Where, now, is their God?"
when our God is in heaven
and all that Adonai wills Adonai accomplishes.
Their idols are silver and gold,
the work of their hands.
They have mouths, but cannot speak;
eyes, but cannot see;
they have ears, but cannot hear;
noses, but cannot smell:
they have hands, but cannot touch;
feet, but cannot walk;
they can make no sound in their throats.
Those who fashion them,
all who trust in them,
shall become like them.
O Israel, trust in Adonai!
Adonai is their help and shield.
O house of Aaron, trust in Adonai!
Adonai is their help and shield.
O you who fear Adonai, trust in Adonai!

Adonai is their help and shield.
Adonai is mindful of us.
Adonai will bless us;
Adonai will bless the house of Israel;
Adonai will bless the house of Aaron;
Adonai will bless those who fear Adonai,
small and great alike.

May Adonai increase your numbers,
yours and your children's also.
May you be blessed by Adonai,
Maker of heaven and earth.
The heavens belong to Adonai,
but the earth Adonai gave over to us.
The dead cannot praise Adonai,
nor any who go down in silence.
But we will bless Adonai
now and forever.
Halleluyah.

PSALM 116

I love Adonai
for Adonai hears my voice, my pleas;
for Adonai turns an ear to me
whenever I call.
The bonds of death encompassed me;
the torments of Sheol overtook me.
I came upon trouble and sorrow
and I invoked the name of Adonai,
"O Adonai, save my life!"

Adonai is gracious and beneficent;
our God is compassionate.
Adonai protects the simple;
I was brought low and Adonai saved me.
Be at rest, once again, O my soul,
for Adonai has been good to you.
You have delivered me from death,
my eyes from tears,
my feet from stumbling.
I shall walk before Adonai
in the lands of the living.
I trust [in Adonai];
out of great suffering I spoke
and said rashly,
"All people are false."

How can I repay Adonai
for all God's bounties to me?
I raise the cup of deliverance
and invoke the name of Adonai.
I will pay my vows to Adonai
in the presence of all God's people.
The death of God's faithful ones
is grievous in God's sight.

Adonai,
I am Your servant,
Your servant, the son of your maidservant;
You have undone the cords that bound me.
I will sacrifice a thank offering to You
and invoke the name of Adonai.
I will pay my vows to Adonai
in the presence of all God's people,
in the courts of the house of Adonai,
in the midst of Jerusalem.
Halleluyah.

PSALM 117

Praise Adonai, all you nations;
extol Adonai, all you peoples,
for great is God's steadfast love toward us;
the faithfulness of Adonai endures forever.
Halleluyah.

PSALM 118

Praise Adonai, for Adonai is good,
God's steadfast love is eternal.
Let Israel declare,
"God's steadfast love is eternal."
Let the house of Aaron declare,
"God's steadfast love is eternal."
Let those who fear Adonai declare,
"God's steadfast love is eternal."

In distress I called on Adonai;
Adonai answered me and brought me relief.
Adonai is on my side,
I have no fear;
what can anyone do to me?

With Adonai on my side as my helper,
I will see the downfall of my foes.

It is better to take refuge in Adonai
than to trust in mortals;
It is better to take refuge in Adonai
than to trust in the great.

All nations have beset me;
by the name of Adonai I will surely cut them down.
They beset me, they surround me;
by the name of Adonai I will surely cut them down.
They beset me like bees;
they shall be extinguished like burning thorns;
by the name of Adonai I will surely cut them down.

You pressed me hard,
I nearly fell;
but Adonai helped me.
Adonai is my strength and my might;
Adonai has become my deliverance.
The tents of the victorious resound with joyous
shouts of deliverance,
"The right hand of Adonai is triumphant!
The right hand of Adonai is exalted!
The right hand of Adonai is triumphant!"

I shall not die but live
and proclaim the works of Adonai.
Adonai punished me severely,
but did not hand me over to death.

Open the gates of victory for me
that I may enter them and praise Adonai.
This is the gateway to Adonai
the victorious shall enter through it.

I praise You, for You have answered me,
and have become my deliverance.
The stone that the builders rejected
has become the chief cornerstone.

This is God's doing;
it is marvelous in our sight.
This is the day that Adonai has made—
let us exult and rejoice on it.
O Adonai, deliver us!
O Adonai, let us prosper!

May who enters be blessed in the name of Adonai;
we bless you from the House of Adonai.
Adonai is God;
Adonai has given us light;
bind the festal offering to the horns of the altar with cords.
You are my God and I will praise You;
You are my God and I will extol You.
Praise Adonai for Adonai is good,
God's steadfast love is eternal.

SUPPLEMENTAL READING

Sequential reading: Read together the third line of each stanza.

AND IT CAME TO PASS AT MIDNIGHT
(*VAY'HI BACHATZI HALAILAH*)

Unto God let praise be brought
For the wonders the Almighty has wrought—
At the solemn hour of midnight.

All the earth was sunk in night
When God said, "Let there be light!"
Thus the day was formed from midnight.

So was primal man redeemed
When the light of reason gleamed
Through the darkness of the midnight.

To the Patriarch, God revealed
The true faith, so long concealed
By the darkness of the midnight.

But this truth was long obscured
By the slavery endured
In the black Egyptian midnight.

Till the messengers of light
Sent by God, dispelled the night,
And it came to pass at midnight.

Then the people God had freed
Pledged themselves God's law to heed,
And it came to pass at midnight.

When they wandered from the path
Of the Lord, God's righteous wrath
Hurled them into darkest midnight.

But the prophets' burning word
By repentant sinners heard
Called them back from darkest midnight.

God a second time decreed
That the people should be freed
From the blackness of the midnight.

Songs of praise to God ascend,
Festive lights their glory lend
To illuminate the midnight.

Soon the night of exile falls
And within the Ghetto walls
Israel groans in dreary midnight.

Anxiously with God they plead,
Who still trust the Almighty's help in need,
In the darkest hour of midnight.

And God hears their piteous cry,
"Wait! Be strong, My help is nigh,
Soon will pass—the long-drawn midnight."

"Tenderly I cherish you
For a service great and true;
When 'tis past—the long-drawn midnight."

O Thou Guardian of the Right,
Lead us onward to the light,
From the darkness of the midnight.

God, let the day appear
When all people Thy name revere
And Thy light dispels the midnight.

When no longer shall the foe
From the oppressed wring cries of woe
In the darkness of the midnight.

But Thy love all hearts shall sway;
And Thy light drive gloom away,
And to midday change the midnight.

ADDITIONAL SONGS

Optional song: A new version by Ben Aronin, sung to the tune of "Clementine."

THE BALLAD OF THE FOUR SONS

Said the father to his children:
"At the seder you will dine,
You will eat your fill of matzah,
You will drink four cups of wine."

Now this father had no daughters,
But his sons numbered four,
One was wise and one was wicked,
One was simple and a bore.

And the fourth was sweet and winsome,
He was young and he was small.
While his brothers asked the questions,
He could scarcely speak at all.

Said the wise son to his father,
"Would you please explain the laws,
Of the customs of the seder,
Will you please explain the cause?"

And the father proudly answered,
"As our fathers ate in speed,
Ate the paschal lamb ere midnight
And from slavery were freed."

So we follow their example
And ere midnight must complete
All the seder, and we should not
After twelve remain to eat.

Then did sneer the son so wicked:
"What does all this mean to you?"
And the father's voice was bitter
As his grief and anger grew.

"If yourself you don't consider
As a son of Israel,
Then for you this has no meaning,
You could be a slave as well."

Then the simple son said simply,
"What is this?" and quietly,
The good father told his offspring,
"We were freed from slavery."

But the youngest son was silent
For he could not ask at all.
His bright eyes were bright with wonder
As his father told him all.

Now dear children heed the lesson
And remember evermore,
What the father told the children,
Told his sons that numbered four.

Optional song: An African American "Spiritual"

 GO DOWN MOSES

When Israel was in Egypt's land,
"Let my people go!"
Oppressed so hard they could not stand,
"Let my people go!"

Go Down, Moses, way down in Egypt's land;
Tell ol' Pharaoh, "Let my people go!"

"Thus saith the Lord," bold Moses said,
"Let my people go!"
If not I'll smite your first born dead.
"Let my people go!"

Go Down, Moses, way down in Egypt's land;
Tell ol' Pharaoh, "Let my people go!"

The Lord told Moses what to do,
"Let my people go!"
To lead the children of Israel through.
"Let my people go!"

Go Down, Moses, way down in Egypt's land;
Tell ol' Pharaoh, "Let my people go!"

When they had reached the other shore,
   "Let my people go!"
They sang a song of triumph o'er.
   "Let my people go!"

Go Down, Moses, way down in Egypt's land;
Tell ol' Pharaoh, "Let my people go!"

WHO KNOWS ONE?

אֶחָד מִי יוֹדֵעַ?   *ECHAD MI YODEI-A*

אֶחָד מִי יוֹדֵעַ?   *Echad mi yodei-a?*
אֶחָד אֲנִי יוֹדֵעַ:   *Echad ani yodei-a:*
אֶחָד אֱלֹהֵינוּ   *Echad Eloheinu*
שֶׁבַּשָּׁמַיִם וּבָאָרֶץ.   *shebashamayim uvaaretz.*

שְׁנַיִם מִי יוֹדֵעַ?   *Sh'nayim mi yodei-a?*
שְׁנַיִם אֲנִי יוֹדֵעַ:   *Sh'nayim ani yodei-a:*
שְׁנֵי לֻחוֹת הַבְּרִית,   *Sh'nei luchot hab'rit,*
אֶחָד אֱלֹהֵינוּ   *Echad Eloheinu*
שֶׁבַּשָּׁמַיִם וּבָאָרֶץ.   *shebashamayim uvaaretz.*

שְׁלוֹשָׁה מִי יוֹדֵעַ?   *Sh'loshah mi yodei-a?*
שְׁלוֹשָׁה אֲנִי יוֹדֵעַ:   *Sh'loshah ani yodei-a:*
שְׁלוֹשָׁה אָבוֹת,   *Sh'loshah Avot,*
שְׁנֵי לֻחוֹת הַבְּרִית,   *Sh'nei luchot hab'rit,*
אֶחָד אֱלֹהֵינוּ   *Echad Eloheinu*
שֶׁבַּשָּׁמַיִם וּבָאָרֶץ.   *shebashamayim uvaaretz.*

אַרְבַּע מִי יוֹדֵעַ?   *Arba mi yodei-a?*
אַרְבַּע אֲנִי יוֹדֵעַ:   *Arba ani yodei-a:*
אַרְבַּע אִמָּהוֹת,   *Arba Imahot,*
שְׁלוֹשָׁה אָבוֹת,   *Sh'loshah Avot,*
שְׁנֵי לֻחוֹת הַבְּרִית,   *Sh'nei luchot hab'rit,*
אֶחָד אֱלֹהֵינוּ   *Echad Eloheinu*
שֶׁבַּשָּׁמַיִם וּבָאָרֶץ.   *shebashamayim uvaaretz.*

חֲמִשָּׁה מִי יוֹדֵעַ?   *Chamishah mi yodei-a?*
חֲמִשָּׁה אֲנִי יוֹדֵעַ:   *Chamishah ani yodei-a:*

102

חֲמִשָּׁה חֻמְשֵׁי תוֹרָה,
אַרְבַּע אִמָּהוֹת,
שְׁלוֹשָׁה אָבוֹת,
שְׁנֵי לֻחוֹת הַבְּרִית,
אֶחָד אֱלֹהֵינוּ
שֶׁבַּשָּׁמַיִם וּבָאָרֶץ.

Chamishah chumshei Torah,
Arba Imahot,
Sh'loshah Avot,
Sh'nei luchot hab'rit,
Echad Eloheinu
shebashamayim uvaaretz.

שִׁשָּׁה מִי יוֹדֵעַ?
שִׁשָּׁה אֲנִי יוֹדֵעַ:
שִׁשָּׁה סִדְרֵי מִשְׁנָה,
חֲמִשָּׁה חֻמְשֵׁי תוֹרָה,
אַרְבַּע אִמָּהוֹת,
שְׁלוֹשָׁה אָבוֹת,
שְׁנֵי לֻחוֹת הַבְּרִית,
אֶחָד אֱלֹהֵינוּ
שֶׁבַּשָּׁמַיִם וּבָאָרֶץ.

Shishah mi yodei-a?
Shishah ani yodei-a:
Shishah sidrei Mishnah,
Chamishah chumshei Torah,
Arba Imahot,
Sh'loshah Avot,
Sh'nei luchot hab'rit,
Echad Eloheinu
shebashamayim uvaaretz.

שִׁבְעָה מִי יוֹדֵעַ?
שִׁבְעָה אֲנִי יוֹדֵעַ:
שִׁבְעָה יְמֵי שַׁבַּתָּא,
שִׁשָּׁה סִדְרֵי מִשְׁנָה,
חֲמִשָּׁה חֻמְשֵׁי תוֹרָה,
אַרְבַּע אִמָּהוֹת,
שְׁלוֹשָׁה אָבוֹת,
שְׁנֵי לֻחוֹת הַבְּרִית,
אֶחָד אֱלֹהֵינוּ
שֶׁבַּשָּׁמַיִם וּבָאָרֶץ.

Shivah mi yodei-a?
Shivah ani yodei-a:
Shivah y'mei shabata,
Shishah sidrei Mishnah,
Chamishah chumshei Torah,
Arba Imahot,
Sh'loshah Avot,
Sh'nei luchot hab'rit,
Echad Eloheinu
shebashamayim uvaaretz.

שְׁמוֹנָה מִי יוֹדֵעַ?
שְׁמוֹנָה אֲנִי יוֹדֵעַ:
שְׁמוֹנָה יְמֵי מִילָה,
שִׁבְעָה יְמֵי שַׁבַּתָּא,
שִׁשָּׁה סִדְרֵי מִשְׁנָה,
חֲמִשָּׁה חֻמְשֵׁי תוֹרָה,
אַרְבַּע אִמָּהוֹת,
שְׁלוֹשָׁה אָבוֹת,
שְׁנֵי לֻחוֹת הַבְּרִית,
אֶחָד אֱלֹהֵינוּ
שֶׁבַּשָּׁמַיִם וּבָאָרֶץ.

Sh'monah mi yodei-a?
Sh'monah ani yodei-a:
Sh'monah y'mei milah,
Shivah y'mei shabata,
Shishah sidrei Mishnah,
Chamishah chumshei Torah,
Arba Imahot,
Sh'loshah Avot,
Sh'nei luchot hab'rit,
Echad Eloheinu
shebashamayim uvaaretz.

תִּשְׁעָה מִי יוֹדֵעַ?	Tishah mi yodei-a?
תִּשְׁעָה אֲנִי יוֹדֵעַ:	Tishah ani yodei-a:
תִּשְׁעָה יַרְחֵי לֵדָה,	Tishah yarchei leidah,
שְׁמוֹנָה יְמֵי מִילָה,	Sh'monah y'mei milah,
שִׁבְעָה יְמֵי שַׁבַּתָּא,	Shivah y'mei shabata,
שִׁשָּׁה סִדְרֵי מִשְׁנָה,	Shishah sidrei Mishnah,
חֲמִשָּׁה חֻמְשֵׁי תוֹרָה,	Chamishah chumshei Torah,
אַרְבַּע אִמָּהוֹת,	Arba Imahot,
שְׁלוֹשָׁה אָבוֹת,	Sh'loshah Avot,
שְׁנֵי לֻחוֹת הַבְּרִית,	Sh'nei luchot hab'rit,
אֶחָד אֱלֹהֵינוּ	Echad Eloheinu
שֶׁבַּשָּׁמַיִם וּבָאָרֶץ.	shebashamayim uvaaretz.

עֲשָׂרָה מִי יוֹדֵעַ?	Asarah mi yodei-a?
עֲשָׂרָה אֲנִי יוֹדֵעַ:	Asarah ani yodei-a:
עֲשָׂרָה דִבְּרַיָּא,	Asarah dib'raya,
תִּשְׁעָה יַרְחֵי לֵדָה,	Tishah yarchei leidah,
שְׁמוֹנָה יְמֵי מִילָה,	Sh'monah y'mei milah,
שִׁבְעָה יְמֵי שַׁבַּתָּא,	Shivah y'mei shabata,
שִׁשָּׁה סִדְרֵי מִשְׁנָה,	Shishah sidrei Mishnah,
חֲמִשָּׁה חֻמְשֵׁי תוֹרָה,	Chamishah chumshei Torah,
אַרְבַּע אִמָּהוֹת,	Arba Imahot,
שְׁלוֹשָׁה אָבוֹת,	Sh'loshah Avot,
שְׁנֵי לֻחוֹת הַבְּרִית,	Sh'nei luchot hab'rit,
אֶחָד אֱלֹהֵינוּ	Echad Eloheinu
שֶׁבַּשָּׁמַיִם וּבָאָרֶץ.	shebashamayim uvaaretz.

אַחַד עָשָׂר מִי יוֹדֵעַ?	Achad asar mi yodei-a?
אַחַד עָשָׂר אֲנִי יוֹדֵעַ:	Achad asar ani yodei-a:
אַחַד עָשָׂר כּוֹכְבַיָּא,	Achad asar koch'vaya,
עֲשָׂרָה דִבְּרַיָּא,	Asarah dib'raya,
תִּשְׁעָה יַרְחֵי לֵדָה,	Tishah yarchei leidah,
שְׁמוֹנָה יְמֵי מִילָה,	Sh'monah y'mei milah,
שִׁבְעָה יְמֵי שַׁבַּתָּא,	Shivah y'mei shabata,
שִׁשָּׁה סִדְרֵי מִשְׁנָה,	Shishah sidrei Mishnah,
חֲמִשָּׁה חֻמְשֵׁי תוֹרָה,	Chamishah chumshei Torah,
אַרְבַּע אִמָּהוֹת,	Arba Imahot,

שְׁלוֹשָׁה אָבוֹת, — Sh'loshah Avot,
שְׁנֵי לֻחוֹת הַבְּרִית, — Sh'nei luchot hab'rit,
אֶחָד אֱלֹהֵינוּ — Echad Eloheinu
שֶׁבַּשָּׁמַיִם וּבָאָרֶץ. — shebashamayim uvaaretz.

שְׁנֵים עָשָׂר מִי יוֹדֵעַ? — Sh'neim asar mi yodei-a
שְׁנֵים עָשָׂר אֲנִי יוֹדֵעַ: — Sh'neim asar ani yodei-a:
שְׁנֵים עָשָׂר שִׁבְטַיָּא, — Sh'neim asar shivtaya,
אַחַד עָשָׂר כּוֹכְבַיָּא, — Achad asar kochvaya,
עֲשָׂרָה דִבְּרַיָּא, — Asarah dib'raya,
תִּשְׁעָה יַרְחֵי לֵדָה, — Tishah yarchei leidah,
שְׁמוֹנָה יְמֵי מִילָה, — Sh'monah y'mei milah,
שִׁבְעָה יְמֵי שַׁבַּתָּא, — Shivah y'mei shabata,
שִׁשָּׁה סִדְרֵי מִשְׁנָה, — Shishah sidrei Mishnah,
חֲמִשָּׁה חֻמְשֵׁי תוֹרָה, — Chamishah chumshei Torah,
אַרְבַּע אִמָּהוֹת, — Arba Imahot,
שְׁלוֹשָׁה אָבוֹת, — Sh'loshah Avot,
שְׁנֵי לֻחוֹת הַבְּרִית, — Sh'nei luchot hab'rit,
אֶחָד אֱלֹהֵינוּ — Echad Eloheinu
שֶׁבַּשָּׁמַיִם וּבָאָרֶץ. — shebashamayim uvaaretz.

שְׁלוֹשָׁה עָשָׂר מִי יוֹדֵעַ? — Sh'loshah asar mi yodei-a?
שְׁלוֹשָׁה עָשָׂר אֲנִי יוֹדֵעַ: — Sh'loshah asar ani yodei-a:
שְׁלוֹשָׁה עָשָׂר מִדַּיָּא, — Sh'loshah asar midaya,
שְׁנֵים עָשָׂר שִׁבְטַיָּא, — Sh'neim asar shivtaya,
אַחַד עָשָׂר כּוֹכְבַיָּא, — Achad asar koch'vaya,
עֲשָׂרָה דִבְּרַיָּא, — Asarah dib'raya,
תִּשְׁעָה יַרְחֵי לֵדָה, — Tishah yarchei leidah,
שְׁמוֹנָה יְמֵי מִילָה, — Sh'monah y'mei milah,
שִׁבְעָה יְמֵי שַׁבַּתָּא, — Shivah y'mei shabata,
שִׁשָּׁה סִדְרֵי מִשְׁנָה, — Shishah sidrei Mishnah,
חֲמִשָּׁה חֻמְשֵׁי תוֹרָה, — Chamishah chumshei Torah,
אַרְבַּע אִמָּהוֹת, — Arba Imahot,
שְׁלוֹשָׁה אָבוֹת, — Sh'loshah Avot,
שְׁנֵי לֻחוֹת הַבְּרִית, — Sh'nei luchot hab'rit,
אֶחָד אֱלֹהֵינוּ — Echad Eloheinu
שֶׁבַּשָּׁמַיִם וּבָאָרֶץ. — shebashamayim uvaaretz.

♫

HATIKVAH

Words: N. H. Imber (adapted)
Music: Samuel Cohen

הַתִּקְוָה   *HATIKVAH*

כָּל־עוֹד בַּלֵּבָב פְּנִימָה,	*Kol od baleivav p'nimah,*
נֶפֶשׁ יְהוּדִי הוֹמִיָּה.	*Nefesh Y'hudi homiyah.*
וּלְפַאֲתֵי מִזְרָח קָדִימָה	*Ulfaatei mizrach kadimah*
עַיִן לְצִיּוֹן צוֹפִיָּה.	*Ayin l'Tziyon tzofiyah.*
עוֹד לֹא אָבְדָה תִּקְוָתֵנוּ,	*Od lo av'dah tikvateinu,*
הַתִּקְוָה בַּת שְׁנוֹת אַלְפַּיִם,	*Hatikvah bat sh'not alpayim,*
לִהְיוֹת עַם חָפְשִׁי בְּאַרְצֵנוּ,	*Lih'yot am chofshi b'artzeinu,*
אֶרֶץ צִיּוֹן וִירוּשָׁלָיִם.	*Eretz Tziyon viY'rushalayim.*

So long as within the inmost heart,
a Jewish spirit sings,
so long as the eye looks eastward,
gazing toward Zion, our hope is not lost,
the hope of two thousand years,
to be a free people in our land,
the land of Zion and Jerusalem.

REFERENCES AND NOTES

The Meaning of the Four Cups of Wine at a Passover Seder

The *Kiddush* cup that holds the wine is our symbol of joy. The wine poured into the cup is our hope for life's sweetness. Together, poured to the brim, the cup stands for the fullness of our days.

FIRST CUP OF WINE

We remember God's promise to our ancestors and to every generation:

> "I will free you from the labors of the Egyptians." (Exodus 6:6)

We drink the first cup of wine to celebrate God's promise of freedom from slavery and oppression. From our enslavement in Egypt we learn that there are times when bitterness is a companion to life's sweetness. The story of our deliverance teaches us that a life touched by God's presence strengthens hope, providing us with the will to overcome the bitter and to rejoice in the sweetness and sanctity of every life.

SECOND CUP OF WINE

We remember God's promise to our ancestors and to every generation:

> "I will deliver you from their bondage." (Exodus 6:6)

We drink the second cup of wine to celebrate the survival of the Jewish people. We remember how, enslaved in Egypt, we retained our identity and integrity as a people—giving us the will to survive, hope for the future, and ultimately, the strength to pursue the freedom promised by God. We remember all the men, women, and children who have fought for freedom from oppression through the generations: from the days of the Exodus, the Spanish Inquisition, the Holocaust, and right up to the present day.

Third Cup of Wine

We remember God's promise to our ancestors and to every generation:

> "I will redeem you with an outstretched arm and with great
> acts of judgment." (Exodus 6:6)

We drink the third cup of wine to celebrate the holiness of our bond to every family member and our connection to all men, women, and children of every religion, race, and creed. May the goodwill in each of us draw us closer to one another, strengthening the ties between us so we may help each other through hard times as well as joyously celebrate good times together.

Fourth Cup of Wine

We remember God's promise to our ancestors and to every generation:

> "I will take you to be My people, and I will be your God."
> (Exodus 6:7)

We dedicate the fourth cup of wine to the meaning of *shalom*—to peace. May the One who broke Pharaoh's yoke forever shatter all fetters of oppression and hasten the day when swords shall, at last, be turned into plowshares and spears into pruning hooks (Isaiah 2:4). May the State of Israel, all peoples in the Middle East, and peoples of all religions, races, and creeds throughout the world soon experience the blessings of peace.

LIST OF ILLUSTRATIONS

LIST OF MUSIC AND SONGS

These following songs can all be found on the accompanying music collection, *Sharing the Journey: A Musical Companion for the Seder.* A CD of this collection can be found in the Leader's Guide to *Sharing the Journey,* and can also be purchased as downloadable MP-3's at on-line music download sites.

ENDNOTES

pp. 1–2: **ASHKENAZI RECIPES** Joan Nathan, *Joan Nathan's Jewish Holiday Cookbook* (New York: Schocken Books, 2004), 332–35.

p. 2: **AN ORANGE** Susannah Heschel, "Orange on the Seder Plate," in *The Women's Passover Companion* (Woodstock, VT: Jewish Lights Publishing, 2003), 70–77.

p. 6: **A MOMENT FOR ADDITIONAL LEARNING** Based on the meaning of leaven and *chameitz* discussed by Rabbi Herbert E. Drooz, Temple Beth Emeth, Wilmington, Delaware, in a Passover sermon, April 1, 1977.

p. 16: **BLESSED ARE YOU** "Blessed are you who come" are traditional words of welcome. They also appear in *The Open Door: A Passover Haggadah*, ed. Sue Levi, Elwell (New York: CCAR Press, 2002), 3.

p. 17: **HINEIH MAH TOV** Sue Horowitz is a songwriter from York, Maine. She wrote a song based upon Psalm 133, *Hineih Mah Tov*. The words to this song are quoted here. Used by permission of Sue Horowitz.

p. 17: **LAMPS OF OUR PEOPLE** "Lamps of our people" refers to an explanation for kindling the lights in a traditional naming ceremony for a newborn baby girl (unattributed), from *Leviticus Rabbah* 31:4.

p. 23: **WASHING OF THE HANDS** The role of water in the story of Passover appears in other Haggadot, including *The Open Door: A Passover Haggadah*, ed. Sue Levi Elwell (New York: CCAR Press, 2002), 23. It is sometimes found with the discussion of Miriam's cup.

p. 27: **KING** Martin Luther King Jr., "The Birth of a New Nation" (sermon, Dexter Avenue Baptist Church, Montgomery, AL, April 7, 1957).

p. 27: **HESCHEL** Abraham Joshua Heschel, *The Insecurity of Freedom: Essays on Human Existence* (New York: Farrar, Straus and Giroux, 1966), 17.

p. 28: **BENEDICTION** The benediction written at Bergen-Belsen is from *Language of Faith: A Selection from the Most Expressive Jewish Prayers*, ed. Nahum N. Glatzer (New York: Schocken Books, 1967), 216.

p. 28: **WIESEL** Elie Wiesel, in *Encountering the Jewish Future: With Wiesel, Buber, Heschel, Arendt, and Levinas*, ed. Marc H. Ellis (Minneapolis: Fortress Press, 2011), 50.

p. 51: **DIVINE HELP** The reference to matzah as "a symbol of divine help" appears in *The Union Haggadah* (Central Conference of American Rabbis, 1923), 36.

p. 54: **PSALM 113, PSALM 114** Adapted from *JPS Tanach* (Philadelphia, PA: Jewish Publication Society, 2003). Used by permission of Jewish Publication Society.

p. 63: **OPENING THE DOOR** The following questions and answers are adapted from the pamphlet "For Your Happy Seder," © Coast Bulletin Publication 1957.

p. 67: **FOURTH CUP OF WINE** The responsive reading prior to the blessing adapted in part from "The Final Benediction," in *The Union Haggadah* (Central Conference of American Rabbis, 1923), 78.

p. 70: **THE HISTORIC VERSION** From *The Union Haggadah* (Central Conference of American Rabbis, 1923).

p. 76: **CHAD GADYA** For references to *Chad Gadya*, see American Conference of Cantors website: www.accantors.org/acc/node/383.

p. 85: **TAKE US OUT OF EGYPT** Attributed to Ron Wolfson, from *Jewish Family Education Passover Haggadah*, © by Rabbi Barry Dov Lerner (Philadelphia: Foundation for Family Education, Inc., 2007).

p. 85: **TAKE ME OUT TO THE SEDER** "Take Me Out to the Seder" appears in several Haggadot. The original source is unknown. New words for the first verse of "Take Me Out to the Seder" written by Alan S. Yoffie.

p. 89: **BIRKAT HAMAZON** *Birkat HaMazon* and transliteration adapted from *Mishkan T'filah: A Reform Siddur*, ed. Elyse D. Frishman (New York: CCAR Press, 2007) 606–9.

pp. 92–94: **PSALMS** From *JPS Tanach* (Philadelphia, PA: Jewish Publication Society, 2003). Used by permission of Jewish Publication Society.

BIBLIOGRAPHY

Materials reviewed for preparation of *Sharing the Journey: The Haggadah for the Contemporary Family* include but are not limited to the following:

The Agam Passover Haggadah. Illustrated by Yaakov Agam. Translated by Moshe Kohn. Jerusalem: Gefen Publishing House, 1993.

Anisfeld, Sharon Cohen, Tara Mohr, and Catherine Spector. *The Women's Seder Sourcebook.* Woodstock, VT: Jewish Lights, 2003.

Arnow, David. *Creating Lively Passover Seders.* 2nd ed. Woodstock, VT: Jewish Lights, 2011.

Bronstein, Herbert, ed. *A Passover Haggadah.* Drawings by Leonard Baskin. New York: CCAR Press, 1982.

Die Pessach Haggadah des Gerschom Kohen, 1527. Facsimile edition by B. Katz and H. Loewe. Berlin, 1925.

Elwell, Sue Levi, ed. *The Open Door: A Passover Haggadah.* Drawings by Ruth Weisberg. New York: CCAR Press, 2002.

"Guide to Passover for Interfaith Couples" and other materials available on www.interfaithfamily.com.

Glatzer, Nahum N., ed. *Language of Faith: A Selection from the Most Expressive Jewish Prayers.* New York: Schocken Books, 1967.

Hoffman, Lawrence A., and David Arnow, eds. *My People's Passover Haggadah.* 2 vols. Woodstock, VT: Jewish Lights, 2008.

The Illustrated Hagada. First Jerusalem Edition. Illustrated by Arieh Al-Hanani. Musical arrangements by Solomon Rosowsky. Jerusalem: Hamadpis Lipshitz Art Printers & Publishers, 1930.

Jerusalem Haggadah. Illustrated by Shmuel Bonneh. Haifa: Shilmona Publishing, 1968.

Kalderon, Asher. *The New Passover Haggadah.* Tel Aviv: A Kalderon Arts, 2008.

Lerner, Barry Dov. *Jewish Family Education Passover Haggadah*. Philadelphia: Foundation For Family Education, Inc., 2007.

Let My People Go: A Haggadah. Illustrated by Mark Podwal. New York: Darien House, 1972.

Mishkan T'filah: A Reform Siddur. Edited by Elyse D. Frishman. New York: CCAR Press, 2007.

The Moriah Haggadah. Illustrated by Avner Moriah. Israel: Har Adar, 2003.

The Moss Haggadah. Illustrated by David Moss. Berkley, CA: Bet Alpha Editions, 2000.

A Night of Questions: A Passover Haggadah. Edited by Joy Levitt and Michael Strassfeld. Illustrated by Jeffrey Schrier. Philadelphia: PA: The Reconstructionist Press, 2000.

A Passover Haggadah. Commented upon by Elie Wiesel and illustrated by Mark Podwal. New York: Simon & Schuster, 1993.

The Passover Haggadah, facsimile edition from Venice 1604. Jerusalem: Makor Publishing, 1974.

Passover Haggadah. Deluxe edition, by Bernard Levy for Maxwell House. New York: Kraft General Foods, 1996.

"Passover Haggadah, Unity Seder." Pesach 5743/1983.

The Pessach Haggadah. Illuminated by Kafra. New York: Feldheim Publishers, 1949.

Raban, Zeev. *The Haggadah*. Tel Aviv: Sinai Publishing, 1967.

Ross, Lesli Koppelman. *Celebrate! The Complete Jewish Holiday Handbook*. Northvale, NJ: Jason Aronson, 1994.

Sacks, Jonathan. *Rabbi Jonathan Sacks's Haggadah*. New York: Continuum, 2006.

The Sarajevo Haggadah, facsimile edition. Beograd: Prosveta, 1983.

Silber, David, with Rachel Furst. *A Passover Haggadah: Go Forth and Learn*. Philadelphia: Jewish Publication Society, 2011.

Silberman, Shoshana. *A Family Haggadah*. Rockville, MD: Kar-Ben, 1987.

Stern, Chaim, ed. *Gates of the House*. New York: CCAR Press, 1977.

The Union Haggadah. Central Conference of American Rabbis, 1923.

The Wolloch Haggadah: Pessach Haggadah in Memory of the Holocaust. Illustrated by David Wander. Calligraphy and micrography by Yonah Weinrib. Haifa: Goldman's Art, 1988.

Zion, Noam, and David Dishon, eds. *The Family Participation Haggadah: A Different Night*. Jerusalem: Shalom Hartman Institute, 1997.

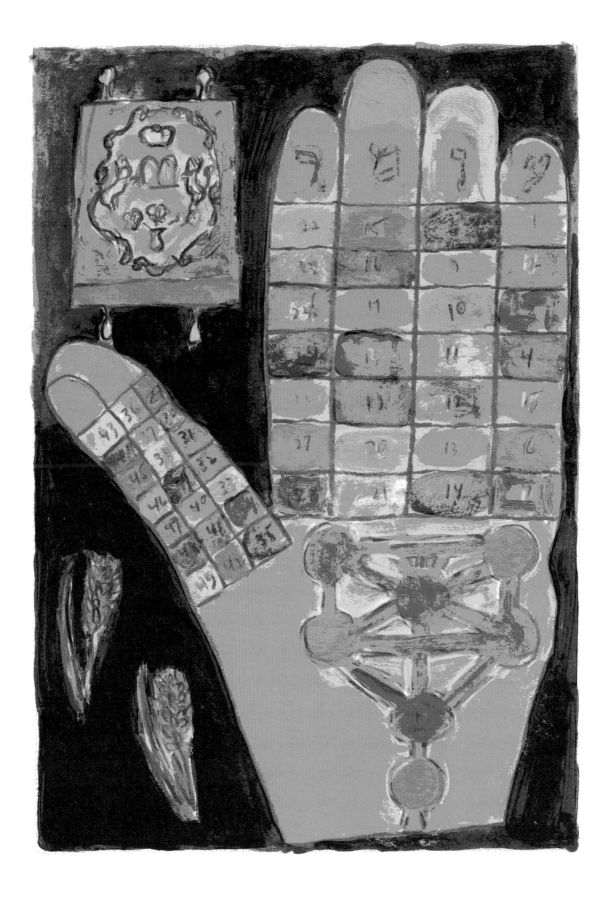

SEDER GUESTS